SECRET
HARROGATE

Paul Chrystal

AMBERLEY

First published 2015

Amberley Publishing
The Hill, Stroud
Gloucestershire, GL5 4EP

www.amberley-books.com

Copyright © Paul Chrystal, 2015

The right of Paul Chrystal to be identified as the
Author of this work has been asserted in accordance
with the Copyrights, Designs and Patents Act 1988.

ISBN 978 1 4456 5253 5 (print)
ISBN 978 1 4456 5254 2 (ebook)

British Library Cataloguing in Publication Data.
A catalogue record for this book is available from the
British Library.

Typesetting by Amberley Publishing.
Printed in Great Britain.

Contents

Introduction

There are of course few secrets left, if any, about a town such as Harrogate with its immense popularity and far-spread fame. The aim of this book is to shine a light on a number of facts, events and features relating to the town which perhaps are less well known and which do not appear so frequently in the many tourist guides and on the myriad websites describing the town. It adumbrates places and happenings which have not enjoyed as much research and publicity as others or, if they have, which may have been forgotten. In the twenty-first century Harrogate remains a place which epitomises style and exudes history, albeit comparatively recent history. It a good place to be and to visit for many reasons, and it is the lesser known, more secret, features of the town which have contributed to that feeling of goodness and well-being just as much as the well known and obvious.

A 1930s guide to Harrogate summed up the town: 'the Mecca of the Ailing, the Playground of the Robust'. That motto still holds good today and still describes well the essence of the place: the people may have changed and the commerce and economy may be very different but, essentially, the town retains many of the features it boasted in its early spa-driven days. This is thanks largely to some inspired commercial foresight and visionary restoration and renovation. *Secret Harrogate* revisits these and reveals some of the town's lesser-known 'secrets'.

Add to this Harrogate Airport; the Brunswick Tunnel and its air-raid shelter; the Victorian gaslit Hales Bar; the Harrogate hoard; Ripley Castle, the non-secret secrets of Menwith Hill, and the economic impact of the 2014 Tour de France and you have a rich tapestry of words and pictures, many of which have been relatively unknown, until now. People, of course, make a place and we meet a diverse range in this book: from William Slingsby and his momentous first sip of the waters; the two famous Bettys: Lupton, veteran guardian of the Pump Room waters and Bettys' Betty, mysterious inspiration for that the name of that most British of tea rooms; and Mr Hak Ng who now is the privileged custodian of the Royal Baths, albeit in a very different environment. The list of visitors and commentators is endless, with Defoe, Celia Fiennes, Lord Byron, Smollet, Dickens and Agatha Christie making cameo appearances along with Elgar, Britten, Parry, Bax and The Beatles, to name but a few more. The book would not be complete with a glance at the secrets harboured by the nearby villages of Goldsborough, Pannal and Ripley.

What I said in my earlier book on the town remains true for this one: 'add to this a walking Debrett's of British aristocracy and European royalty and the book comes alive with literary, musical and historical anecdotes matched only by the very real stories which local firms like Bettys & Taylors, Farrah's and Ogden's live on to tell us.'

Paul Chrystal, October 2015
www.paul.chrystal.com

Very much like the expression on the faces of your husband and daughter at the said times

BG

1. Harrogate as a World Spa

Harrogate Spa and the Devil

The satanic verses from this 1905 card read:

> As Satan was flying over Harrogate Well, /His senses were charmed with the heat and
> the smell, /Says he 'I don't know in what region I roam/But I guess from the smell I'm
> not far from home.' /When Old Betty called after him 'Satan I say, /You were might
> pleased with your journey today; /Pray stay till I've done and we'll both go together. /
> For I'm heartily tired of this changeable weather'. /But Satan well knew if for Betty he
> stayed, /His journey going home would be delayed, /For Harrogate waters such wonders
> can do/That the Devil himself is often robbed of his due.

In 1399 Harrogate became Crown property when the possessions of the Duchy of
Lancaster merged with the English Royal Crown. Until the beginning of the nineteenth
century it may surprise visitors to the town to learn that Harrogate was much smaller
than next-door Knaresborough; at the end of the 1690s it had fifty-seven houses
compared to Knaresborough's 156. Harrogate does not appear in the Domesday Book
and we have to wait until 1332 before its first historical reference, as part of the roll for

The devil comes to Harrogate.

Knaresborough Court. The name comes from the Norse 'Here gatte', the road to Harlow, or to Haverah, which in turn means the road to the soldier's hill. Haverah was a royal park dating back to 1100.

To add to the confusion and uncertainty, *Thorpe's Early History of Harrogate*, published in 1891, tells us that,

> Harrogate is derived from the ancient British of Heywray–gate, i.e., Hey a forest, park, or moor–wray, a brook or stream – and gate, a road. Another fixes the derivation as Harw–gate, the road of robbers ... The titles with which Harrogate has been credited are so innumerable, as to suggest imperfect orthography as their source. The name may still be found in some old established railway guides as 'Harrowgate'; though the w is fast losing its hold upon the heretofore confident railway tabulators. It may not be uninteresting to state that the following, besides the above mentioned, are said to have done duty in turn: 'Harloo–cum-Bylton Banks,' 'Harlowgate', 'Harrogat', 'Harry-gate', and 'Harrowgait'.

In the Middle Ages the waters of nearby St Mungo's and St Robert's were credited with miraculous powers. After the mineral springs were discovered and popularised the population exploded and was at 1,500 by 1810. Harrogate spa water contains much-coveted iron, sulphur and common salt.

There are eighty-eight wells within just two miles of the Royal Pump Room Museum; Harrogate has been called 'The Queen of Inland Watering Places' and 'England's Premier Spa'. But not by the people of Bath ...

Down in one ... then off to Hales round the corner for more (or less) of the same.

2—Here goes !
DRINKING THE WATERS AT HARROGATE.

The Chalybeate Well

'Chalybeate' is derived from the Latin word for steel, *chalybs*, which in turn comes from the Greek χάλυψ, *khálups*. The Chalybes were a mythical people living on Mount Ida in northern Asia Minor who invented iron-working. It all started with Dudley North, who discovered the chalybeate spring at Tunbridge Wells in 1606. North's doctor claimed that the waters contained 'vitriol' and the waters of Tunbridge Wells could cure 'the colic, the melancholy, and the vapours; it made the lean fat, the fat lean; it killed flat worms in the belly, loosened the clammy humours of the body, and dried the over-moist brain.' The English physician Thomas Sydenham (1624–1689), father of British medicine, prescribed chalybeate waters for hysteria.

The Tewit Well

The Tuewhit, or Tewitt, Well itself gets its name from its association in pre-Roman times with the pagan god Teut, according to the 1922 introduction to Dr Edmund Deane's 1626 classic work *Spadacrene Anglica*, or *The English Spaw Fountaine* – 'the earliest and most indispensable source of the history of the waters of Harrogate'. Deane was a prominent York physician. Mr (not Sir, who was his nephew) William Slingsby's discovery of the strange rusty looking waters of the Iron Spring (Tewit) Well in 1571 marked the birth of Harrogate as a world-famous spa town. Deane tells us that Slingsby brought the new-found asset to the attention of Queen Elizabeth's physician, Dr Timothy Bright. Bright, on drinking the water, 'found it in all things to agree with those at the Spaw' – namely, the two famous medicinal springs of Sauveniere and Pouhon at Spa in Belgium – which happened at the time to be a den of Catholicism from which the English Crown was trying to deter its more adventurous subjects from visiting. Finding a spa in Harrogate (the first English town to be designated as a spa) was a godsend, and from then on Harrogate's reputation was assured. Another link, albeit tenuous, between Spa and Harrogate is that Swan Hotel refugee, Agatha Christie's fictional detective, Hercule Poirot was born in Belgian Spa. The well inherited the 1808 Tuscan columned temple which was originally at the Royal Pump Room and designed by Thomas Chippendale; it was closed in 1971 – 400 years after its opening.

That the water here was good for you, Dr Deane was in no doubt:

> Moreover, it clenseth, and purifieth the whole masse of blood contained in the veynes, by purging it from the seresity peccant, and from cholericke, phlegmaticke, and melancholike humours; and that principally by urine, which passeth through the body very cleare, and in great quantity, leaving behind it the minerall forces, and vertues. Their stooles, who drinke of it, are commonly of a blackish, or dark greene colour, partly because it emptieth the liver and splen from adult humours, and melancholy, or the sediment of blood: but more especially, because the mineralls intermixed doe produce and give such a tincture.

Indeed, a positive panacea, the perfect purgative:

> It sheweth divers and sundry other manifest effects and qualities in evacuating the noxious humours of the body, for most part by urine especially when there is any

obstruction about the kidneyes, ureters and bladder: Or by urine and stoole both, if the mesentery, liver, or splen, chance to bee obstructed. But, if the affect or griefe be in the matrix or womb, then it clenseth that way according to the accustomed and usuall manner of women. In melancholike people it purgeth by provoking the hæmorrhoides, and in cholericke by siege, or stoole. If it causeth either vomit or sweat, it is very seldome and rare.

And so on, and on, with psychological as well as physical benefits:

It is also good and availeable against inveterate headaches, migrims, turnings, and swimmings of the head and braine, dizzinesse, epilepsie, or falling sicknesse, and the like cold and moist diseases of the head. It cheereth and reviveth the spirits, strengtheneth the stomacke, causeth a good and quicke appetite, and furthereth digestion. It helpeth the blacke and yellow Jaundisse, and the evill, which is accompanied with strange feare and excessive sadnesse without any evident occasion, or necessary cause, called Melancholia Hypochondria.

Even sexually transmitted infections and women's periods had no hiding place from the beneficent waters:

It shall not bee needfull to speake much of the profit, which will ensue by the fit administration of it in the inveterat venereous Gonorrhæa, causing it to cease and stay totally, and correcting the distemper, and the evill ulcerous disposition of the seed vessels, & the vicine parts. There are very few infirmities properly incident to women, which this water may not seeme to respect much. The use whereof ... is singular good against the greene sicknesse, and also very commodious and behoovefull to procure their monthly evacuation's.

St John's Well

St John's Well, or the Sweet Spaw, was discovered in 1631 by Michael Stanhope of York and was soon joined by a 'necessary house' (toilets), thus providing a very early precursor of a roadside service station. The medical profession generally, and Stanhope in particular in his 1632 *Cures Without Care*, promoted the benefits of these waters: claims grew that they helped in the treatment of indigestion, flatulence, 'hysterical affections' and alcoholism. For many years it was the most popular of Harrogate's chalybeate wells. The first pump room here was built in 1788 by local Alexander Wedderburn. Not everyone, though, was happy: this from Dr Short in his 1740 *History of Mineral Waters* – 'the rendezvous of wantonness and not seldom mad frolics ... luxury, intemperance, unseasonable hours, idleness, gratification of taste are becoming so fashionable ... now it's become so chargeable.' The waters were attracting the wrong sort of people, but they had money ... Whether he was genuinely concerned that his colleagues' good work was being undone by the apparent decadence or whether he was just moaning about the prices remains unclear. The well closed in 1973.

The author of the 1813 *Guide to All the Watering and Sea-Bathing Places* was less than complimentary:

Harrowgate water tastes like rotten eggs and gunpowder; and though it is probable that no person ever made a trial of such a mixture, the idea it conveys is not inapplicable ... While some places are visited because they are fashionable, and others on account of the beauty of their scenery, Harrowgate possesses neither of those attractions in a superior degree, and therefore is chiefly resorted to by the valetudinary, who frequently quaff health from its springs, else we cannot suppose that upwards of two thousand persons annually visit this sequestered spot ... it lies ... on a dreary common.

How things were to change ...

Montpellier

Established in 1835 by Joseph Thackwray, who also owned Montpellier Gardens and the Crown Hotel, 6,000 individual baths were taken here in the 1839 season and for many years Montpellier was considered the best baths in town; they specialised in needle shower and douche baths and invalid Sitz baths. Six new wells, including the famous Kissingen Well, were discovered when the foundations were being dug – no doubt Thackwray was rubbing his hands with glee. The small octagonal building which survives was originally a gatehouse and ticket office for the hotel's gardens. The Montpellier Baths included a suite of Turkish baths: 'First class Turkish baths for gentlemen: 2/6d'.

In 1835 Johnathan Shutt Junior, owner of the Old Swan Hotel, discovered that his neighbour Thackwray intended to build a well yielding sulphur water, and to drain the flow of the public well. Because of this and other acts of vandalism to the wells, the Harrogate Improvements Act of 1841 was approved. Local senior citizens and local hoteliers petitioned for an Act of Parliament to create a body of Improvement Commissioners to ensure that nobody pirated the precious waters in future.

The Magnesia Pump Room

This Gothic-style building was built by the Improvement Commissioners in 1858 in Bogs Field before it was incorporated into the Valley Gardens. Welcomed on account of its milder waters (today it would be branded Sulfur Lite), the Magnesia site is now occupied by a cafeteria. By the mid-nineteenth century the waters of Low Harrogate had become more popular than their High Harrogate neighbours', which explains the plethora of baths down the hill. All very different from the early days when, as Deane told us in 1626, 'the vulgar sort drinke these waters to expelle reefe and felon; yea many who are much troubled with itches, scabs, morphews, ring-worme, and the like are soone holpen.' The Magnesia Well closed in 1973.

New Victoria Baths

Built at the behest of the Harrogate Improvement Commissioners in 1871 on the site of the 1834 Old Victoria Baths, they were originally called the John Williams'

The Magnesia Well in 1910.

Baths after the owner. The commissioners used the upper floor in the central block as offices for a while; they were succeeded by the council after 1884 and then, when the baths closed in the 1920s, the building was later converted into a town hall, the council chamber of which is today virtually in the same place as it was at the time of the commissioners.

The Royal Pump Room

The Royal Pump Room dates from 1842 and was built under the auspices of the newly formed Improvement Commissioners, who were empowered to provide a suitable building to house the Sulphur Well – the world's strongest sulphur well; the original cover was moved to the Tewit Well where it survives today.

The Pump Room was designed by Isaac Shutt and cost £3,000. Stanhope was the first to differentiate between the clientele at the different wells, describing those here as 'the vulgar sort' and questioned the standards of hygiene when 'it was open for the promiscuous of all sorts ... so that the poor Lazar [the leprous] impotent people do dayly environ it, whose putrid rags lie scattered ... it is to be doubted whether they do wash their soares and cleanse their besmirched clouts, though unseen, where diverse persons after dippe their cups and drinke.'

The Royal Pump Room, a distinctive octagonal building was opened to replace the earlier building that had covered the popular Old Sulphur Well. Sheltered from the elements, and at a charge, the water was served in a glass and customers could enjoy musical entertainments while they strolled around the building. For the poor, among whom there was a demand for the sulphur water, a free tap was provided outside the

The Royal Pump Room in 1928.

The Pump Room; a museum since 1953.

building. This tap is still there today. It seems that leprosy patients were tolerated when the well was open to the elements but when it was closed in they were no longer welcome.

In 1842, Harrogate had 3,778 drinkers; in 1867 it was 11,626; in 1925 259,000 were taking the waters. The established daily routine at the Pump Room was as follows: patients arrived between 7 a.m. and 9 a.m. and drank one or more glasses of water, after which they would join the promenaders outside where they would shop, gossip and hear music before taking breakfast (A. B. Granville, *Spas of England*, 1841, p. 52).

The quantity drunk, at one time, should be such that during fifteen minutes' walk, which is to elapse between one dose and the next, the stomach may nearly have got rid of the first before it receives the second.

Afterwards, the chronically sick would have hot bath treatments. Doctors recommended that the basic length of 'the cure' should be at least three weeks. In the early days, waters would have been collected by hotel staff for their residents and brought back to the hotel for them to bathe in.

A Dr Thorp analysed the waters here:

Proven to be beneficial in most forms of Indigestion; Constipation, Flatulence and Acidity. For all cases of functional disorders of the liver. For stimulating the action of the kidneys and in all forms of Chronic Skin Diseases. To be drunk warm or cold. Dosage between 10 and 24 ounces to be taken early in the morning.

Betty Lupton

The Latin inscription on the Pump Room is *Arx celebris fontibus*: the old town motto at its 1884 Charter of Incorporation means 'the town famous for its springs'. Old Betty – Queen of the Well – served the 'strong sulphur' water at the Old Sulphur Well for over sixty years before her death in 1843.

The Royal Baths

The 1841 Harrogate Improvement Act was a catalyst for change when Harrogate shrugged off its provincial, rather unsophisticated ambience and image and set out to rival trend-setting Bath and the other great spas Europe could offer.

In 1887, the corporation took the plunge and sent its surveyor across the Channel to report on the European spa situation, not least at Belgium's Spa and Germany's Baden-Baden. On his return the surveyor's initial response was to upgrade the Victoria Baths but, in the event, the inspired decision was to build a completely new baths which came to be called the Royal Baths. To ensure they got it absolutely right, the corporation held an international competition: twenty-six sets of plans were submitted, with Messrs Baggallay and Bristowe of London the winners. Some of the proposed features, such as the domed pump room, were later cut in order to keep down the cost, but the magnificent building still featured a glazed winter garden, domed entrance hall and numerous treatment rooms, all designed to make these baths the finest hydrotherapy centre in Europe.

It was built on the site of Oddy's 1819 Saline Chalybeate Pump Room, itself constructed on the Kissingen Well. So as not to lose custom during the building of the new baths, the corporation demolished the Montpellier Baths in two stages, the original Turkish baths remaining in operation until the new ones were ready for use. The Royal Baths cost of around £120,000 and were officially opened by HRH The Duke of Cambridge on 23 July

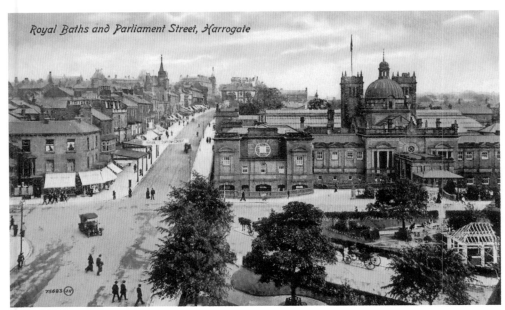

Royal Baths and Parliament Street, Harrogate

The Royal Baths.

1897. The baths gained a new wing in 1898 for the Peat and Plombieres Baths – the latter for the very popular Plombieres two-way system or Harrogate Intestinal Lavage system – a colonic irrigation treatment which could reputedly result in the rapid loss of ½ stone in weight.

Pike's history of Harrogate tells us that at the time, the bathrooms in the Turkish baths were 'of solid glazed brickwork in beautiful tints and patterns' and that the floors were laid in oak parquet or 'in marble mosaic specially designed', (*Pike's Illustrated Account of Harrogate: Its Baths, Activities and Entertainments* (Brighton 1896) p. 23). Likewise, Cyril Baggallay described his design, and captures the ambience, of the Turkish Baths in a lecture on 15 September at the Sanitary Congress in Leeds:

> The south-east corner of the site is occupied by a Turkish bath ... It accommodates about twenty-two persons, and care has been taken to provide a good supply of fresh air, which is heated in a Crumblehulme's furnace. There is also a good cold plunge. The hot rooms, lavatories, and so on, are lined with coloured glazed bricks. On the south-west is a series of special rooms, an inhalation room where people can sit about and read, or amuse themselves while inhaling the vapour, produced by a hot, mineral water fountain; a pulverisation room, fitted with little marble tables, on which are delicate instruments for spraying the eyes, nostrils, throat and ears; and a suite of massage rooms.

Reported in 'The Royal Baths at Harrogate' /
Cyril Baggallay, Journal of Balneology and Climatology
(July 1897), pp.347–55.

Staff at the Royal Baths in 1910. The card boasts that treatments for muco-membranous colitis, chronic appendicitis, etc. are available.

Relaxing at the Royal
Baths in the 1930s.

As well as the Turkish baths, there were more than a dozen other types of bath, douche, or treatments available, along with various types of mineral water. Some of the treatments available were: sulphur baths, for the treatment of rheumatism or eczema; fango treatment, where a form of mud pack was applied to affected joints; and deep pool therapy, in which the patient could exercise while in a hydrotherapy pool. The baths opened from 7.00 a.m. till 8.00 p.m. on weekdays in the summer, with shorter hours in the winter.

Women bathers had special days and, unlike many Turkish baths at the time they were open on Sunday mornings. From November to May, a Turkish bath cost 3/- and 3/6 from June to October. A massage cost 2/- for the first fifteen minutes, and 1/6 for each additional ¼ hour.

The three hot rooms were kept warm at temperatures of 120, 180, and 210 degrees Fahrenheit. If it was wet outside, the advice was, after removing one's shoes, 'to ask the attendant to put them in a warm place so that they may be dry and comfortable when put on again.'

According to the council's rather formal *Handbook to Harrogate*, beginning with a shower, the bather sat down in the first hot room, 'upon which the attendant will spread his towel'. While lying down in the hottest room,

> The attendant will bring a tumblerful of cold water; if not, it should be asked for, or taken from the tap. If there is any fulness in the head, or faintness, the bathman should be summoned by clapping the hands. If the feet are cold, the bathman will douche them with hot water, and some bathers may with advantage have a hot needle bath; indeed, for any disagreeable symptoms the bathman should be consulted, and from his immense experience he will probably know the appropriate remedy. The bather was then summoned to the shampooing room where 'he reclines on a marble slab, upon which the bathman places the towel.

Towels also covered specially shaped wooden rests to support the bather's head and ankles.

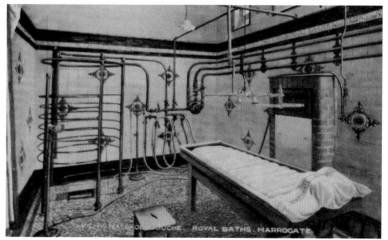

Hot air treatment;
(Greville system);
Vichy massage and
ladies dressing hall in
the Royal Baths.

For many, a Turkish bath must have seemed exotic and mystical; as such it attracted much humour, even among aficionados: for example this article describing the whole rigmarole and titled 'A Yorkshireman Takes his First Turkish Bath' appeared in *The Harrogate Herald* of 8 March 1933 under the nom-de-plume 'Chronicler':

So, first, he warmed t 'slab wi' a bucket of 'ot water. Then 'e says, 'Sit dahn here, sir.' So Ah sat dahn. An' 'e got hold of my arms – first one, then t' other – an' rubbed them up an' dahn. Then he did t' same wi' my legs. Then 'e says 'Lie on yer back, please.' An' he started an' pummelled me wi' his fingers an' thumbs, right from my neck dahn ter my feet. Then he says 'Turn over, please.' An' 'e'd got mi 'ed in a sort o' wooden block, which mi neck just fitted in. An' Ah began ti think of t' guillotine. But t' shampooer said 'You're all right,' an' 'e 'elped me to turn over, so as Ah shouldn't slip off t' slab like. The 'e started pummellin' and rubbin' me again, right from mi neck to mi feet. 'My word,' he says, 'it's coming out of you.'

Then 'e put 'is 'and dahn mi spine an' started hammerin' me. 'There,' he says, 'that rouses your liver.' Then 'e got a sort of loofah scrubbing brush, soaped it well wi some pine soap (it did smell grand), an' 'e scrubbed me dahn proper – it wor grand. Then 'e says, 'Sit up, please.' But 'e 'ad to 'elp me, for Ah wor covered wi soap. Then 'e scrubbed me all down mi front from top ti toe, an' got a bucket of warm watter an' threw it over me—a reg'lar dowsin'. By, Ah did feel fit after it!

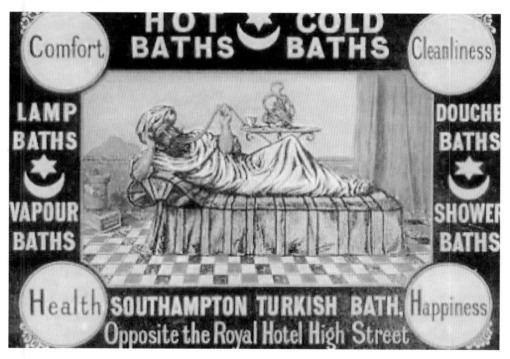

A traditional image of Turkish baths – this is advertisement for the Southampton Turkish Baths in Regent Street. They were opened by John Rose in 1870 and were later bought by the Southampton Turkish Baths Co. Ltd, who resold them in 1880 to a new company with the same name. They closed in 1886.

It should be remembered that the shower would have been a novel experience for many visitors at a time when only public bathing or washing was available.

The baths were extended first in 1909 and 1911 and again in 1939 to include a new treatment wing, panelled lounge hall and the open-air fountain court. Used by the National Health Service from 1949 until 1968, they were then given over to private patients for a short period. From 1969 only the Turkish Sauna suite was in operation, but it remains without question one of the most beautiful of England's last remaining Victorian baths.

The Royal Baths offered around ninety different treatments, catering for a wide range of disorders and diseases – real and imagined. For many of these treatments Harrogate and the Royal Baths in particular became a centre of excellence with an international reputation. Perhaps the most famous was the Saline Sulphur Bath which comprised two waters: Saline Sulphur and Alkaline Sulphur Water – the latter used in the treatment of skin disorders; the former for gout, rheumatism and liver disease. The Nasal Douche and Throat Sprays involved using a medical device which enabled the patient to inhale atomised mineral water to remove mucous attached to the inside of the nose thus, apparently, helping to restore circulation and secretions. The beautiful fountain which stood there is now in the Royal Pump Museum.

Peat baths were also very popular in the Royal Baths – there were four of them: Mineral Peat Bath, the Brine Bath, the Electric Bath and the Ordinary Peat Bath. The minerals for these were brought in from the nearby North York Moors. The baths themselves were made of Burmese teak and took one week to make. Peat baths were efficacious in cases of rheumatism, lumbago, sciatica and the like.

Refurbishment of the Royal Baths was completed in March 2002 as the Royal Turkish Baths Sauna Suite and included a new entrance to the Turkish baths off Parliament Street with the addition of seven treatment rooms and a spa room. A covered atrium was also created as an area for light refreshments and a link between the treatment rooms, which can now be accessed without disturbing people using the Turkish baths. In the UK, only seven such baths remain which date back to the nineteenth century. Three of the seven, including Harrogate, are in England (the Victorian Health Suite in Carlisle and the Health

The grand entrance to the Pump Room Museum in 2015.

An exhibit in the Pump Museum.

The Royal Baths gardens in 1916.

Hydro in Swindon are the others). But none of them is as historically complete and in full working order as Harrogate's. Their importance lies in their unique, resplendent decoration. None of them retains the historical integrity, or are in as full working order, as Harrogate's Turkish Baths. But the website says it best: http://www.yorkshire.com/view/attractions/harrogate/turkish-baths-health-spa-157019:

> At Harrogate's Turkish Baths & Health Spa, amidst surroundings that are pure Victorian, The Baths' Moorish design with great vaults and arches soar to a high arabesque ceiling ornately decorated with colourful stencilled design. The walls are of expertly rendered vibrant glazed brickwork, while underfoot the picture is completed with elaborately assembled mosaic and marble terrazzo floors, all adding to its historic fantasy qualities. For the interior fittings, Victorian dark wood blends with Islamic designs in a beautiful embodiment of Orientalist fusion. But this is a building to be used, not just admired.

Royal Bath Hospital

The 150-bed Royal Bath Hospital and Rawson Convalescent home in Cornwall Road were built in 1889 at a cost of £50,000 on the site of the original forty-bed Bath Hospital which dated from 1824. The purpose of the Royal Bath was to cater for poorer patients who could not afford to pay for typical Harrogate treatments, and who lived at least three miles out of town. In 1931, 1,700 cases from all over the UK were treated. Originally no waters were available on site and patients had to go to places like the Royal Baths to take the cure. The hospital closed in 1994 but not before

A splendid triumphal arch erected in 1889 to celebrate the opening of the Royal Bath Hospital on the Skipton Road; it was attended by Prince Albert Victor, Duke of Clarence.

it had won a reputation as a centre of excellence for the treatment of rheumatoid diseases and as a leading hospital for hydropathic treatments; it is now the Sovereign Court residential development.

Northern Police Orphanage

This was first called the Northern Police Orphanage, and was located in St George's House on Otley Road, Harrogate. It was founded in 1898 by Catherine Gurney, the Quaker social reformer, for the care and welfare of Northern Police Force children who had lost one or both parents. From January 1898 when the first child, Minnie Smith from Sunderland, was admitted, until closure in 1956, 644 children had passed through St George's House. Gurney died in 1930 and at her request was buried at All Saints Church Cemetery, Harlow Hill.

Northern Police Convalescent Home

Next on Catherine Gurney's agenda of reform and rehabilitation in 1901 was the Northern Police Convalescent Home, located on part of the original St George's twelve acres. This opened in 1903 and by 1903 had treated 12,644 patients; it continues to provide care for the police force to this day, under the name St Andrew's Convalescent Home.

Heatherdene Convalescent Home in 1960. Sunderland Royal Infirmary in the nineteenth century had a system of sending patients to convalescent homes; they persuaded the Victoria Hall Disaster Fund to fund the purchase and conversion of Heatherdene Convalescent Home in Lancaster Park, Harrogate. The fund donated £4,000 and the home was opened on 15 September 1892. At its opening it was principally for the admission of children (and some women) but an extension for adults was planned when funds allowed in 1894. In 1914, the home was used as a military hospital until 1919.

Voltaic Cages

The Voltaic Cage Bath emitted pulses of electricity effective in the treatment of patients with polio and MS. The uniform of the female attendants was a long bottle-green skirt, white blouse, large apron and a cap. Men wore a collar and tie and a jacket, which, in the temperatures involved, must have been insufferable. The laconium was heated to 79 degrees Fahrenheit and the caldarium a cool, by comparison, 55 degrees. One of the attendant's crucial jobs was to wipe the brows of clients lest the steaming water scalded their eyes. There were twenty women attendants and three men: because women were unable to undress themselves (the buttons on their dresses being at the back) each lady needed their own attendant.

The Prescribed Routine

The basic recommended length for the 'cure' was for a period of not less than three weeks for 'permanent benefit to be gained':

> 7 a.m.–8 a.m. – Rise and visit pump room for first tumbler of water.
> 7 a.m.–8.15 a.m. – Walk about, listening to the band.
> 8.15 a.m. – Take second tumbler of water.

8.15 a.m–9.00 a.m. – Listen to the band and if prescribed take third glass of water.

9.00 a.m. – Breakfast.

For some people it is advisable that they drive; either by omnibus, carriage, or bath chair but the walk home can be advantageous if it can be accomplished without undue fatigue. Care should be taken to avoid exertion.

10.00 a.m.–11.00 a.m. – Morning paper or letter writing.

11.00 a.m. – Shopping/Walk/Listen to band/or Bathe.

11.30 a.m. – Second visit to Pump Room.

1.00 p.m. – Rest for half an hour.

1.30 p.m. – Lunch to be followed by one hour of rest.

Afternoon Driving, Walking, Cycling, Golfing or third visit to Pump Room. Afternoon tea in Gardens listening to the band.

7.00 p.m. – Dinner.

Concert room
Possibly an opportunity for some to undo all the good that the day had achieved, what with wine, port, cigarettes, cigars and a hearty Yorkshire dinner. Who knows?

The Treatments
This brochure shows very clearly the breathtaking plethora of treatments that were available for all manner of complaints. Available at: http://www.harrogatepeopleandplaces. info/publications/brochures/harrogate1920/listoftreatments.htm:

The beautiful water jug, by the French ceramist Auguste Jean, presented to the Royal Baths in 1873.

Town Brochure for the Season 1920–21
Lists of Treatments

Royal Baths

Balneological

Sulphur Bath – Sulphur Douche – Sulphur Bath and Needle – Sulphur Bath (Beckwith) – Schnaibach Chalybeate – Still Sitz Bath – Running Sitz Bath – Douche or Needle Plain – Carbonic Acid Sulphur – Carbonic Acid Plain – Vapour with Needle or Shower – Turkish – Russian with Needle – Berthallot – Harrogate Massage Douche (Aix System) – Vichy Douche – Berthe and Needle – Berthe and Vichy Douche – Peat ('Moor' or 'Mud') Bath (Plain) – Peat ('Moor' or 'Mud') Bath (Mineral) – Peat ('Moor' or 'Mud') Bath (Brine) – Peat ('Moor' or 'Mud') Bath (Electric) – Peat, Local – Electric Beckwith Sulphur Bath – Electric (Plain Water) Bath – Harrogate Intestinal Douche – Tivoli Douche – Plombieres, Tivoli, and Immersion – Scotch Douche – Special Douche – Thermal Sulphur – Whirlpool Bath with Simultaneous Massage – Oxygen Bath (Mineral Water) – Oxygen Bath (Plain Water) – Pine Bath (Mineral Water) – Pine Bath (Plain Water) – Aeration Bath (Mineral Water) – Aeration Bath (Plain Water).

Accessory Treatments

Harrogate Throat, Nasal, Ear, and Inhalation Treatment – Liver or Peat Pack, with Needle or Douche – 'Fango' Pack – Massage, Swedish, &c. – Massage and Chiropody Outside Baths – Massage and Medical Gymnastics – Swedish and Orthopaedic Exercises – Paraffin Wax Bath – Zander-Borderel Exercises.

Electrical Treatments

D'Arsanval, High Frequency – D'Arsanval, High Frequency with Massage – Harrogate Hot Air Treatment – Dowsing Radiant Heat Bath – Harrogate Combined Light and Heat Bath, followed by a Needle Bath – Schnee Four-Cell Treatment – Catephoresis – Faradism and Galvanism – Diathermy, or Thermo-Penetration – Bergonie Treatment – Static Treatment – Electrical Vibratory Treatment – X-Ray Photograph – Simpson 'S' Ray – Harrogate Bergonie Treatment (for Obesity, &c.) – Bristow Treatment – Berthollet, Cataphoresis, and High Frequency – Bertltollet and Cataphoresis.

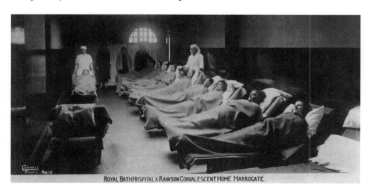

ROYAL BATH HOSPITAL & RAWSON CONVALESCENT HOME HARROGATE.

Royal Bath Hospital patients.

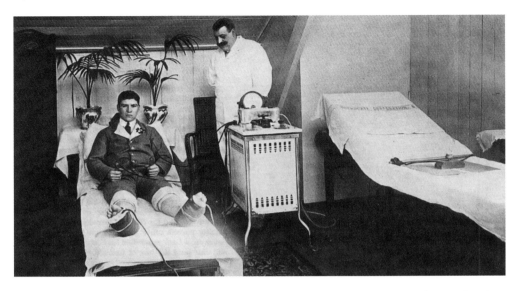

A wounded soldier, one of 100,000 in Harrogate altogether, receiving treatment at the Royal Baths.

Victoria Baths

Thermal Sulphur Bath – Thermal Sulphur Bath and Needle – Sulphur Bath – Electric Water Bath (Plain) – Electric Water Bath (Sulphur) – Electric Water Bath (Brine) – Alkaline Sulphur (Starbeck Water) – Harrogate Oxygen Sulphur Bath – Sulphur Bath and Needle – Douche and Needle – Harrogate Massage Douche (Aix System) – Vichy Douche – Carbonic Acid Bath (Sulphur Water) – Carbonic Acid Bath (Plain Water) – Ascending Douche – Liver Pack – Brine Bath – Douche or Needle – Berthollet Treatment – Massage – Plain Water Bath – Berthollet and Cataphoresis – Cataphoresis Treatment.

Prince of Wales Baths (Starbeck)

Alkaline Sulphur Bath – Massage and Sulphur Bath – Swimming Bath (Plain Water).

Harlow Car Baths

Harlow Car Alkaline Sulphur Bath – Harlow car Alkaline Sulphur Bath and Massage.

Swimming Baths (Skipton Road)

Swimming Bath (Plain Water).

Bottled Medicinal Waters

Patients desiring to continue their 'cure' after they leave Harrogate, can have sent to them the particular Waters they require. If for any reason also the Patient cannot visit

Harrogate, the Waters will of course be forwarded on request. It however need hardly be pointed out that although these Waters are always freshly bottled, yet they are but 'the next best thing' to taking them at their actual sources.

Orders can be left by Patients at any of the Ticket Offices at the Pump Rooms or The Royal Baths; or if sent by post (with remittance to cover) they should be addressed to The General Manager, Wells and Baths Department.

The charges are as follows: per doz. Bottles.

Strong Sulphur (on Medical Prescription only)
Mild Sulphur (on Medical Prescription only)
Magnesia Water   12oz 8/-
Kissingen Water (still) 24oz 12/6
Beckwith Water
No. 36 Well Sulphur
Saline
Aerated Kissingen   8 oz. 7/6
Chloride of Iron   8 oz. 10/6

The Winter Gardens and promenading.

2. Talking About Harrogate

Celia Fiennes

Celia Fiennes was the first woman to visit every county in England; she came to Harrogate on that grand tour – a journey she made on horseback and frequently accompanied by only one or two servants. This is how she described the Old Sulphur Well during her Great Journey to Newcastle and to Cornwall in 1698:

There is the Sulpher or Stincking spaw, not Improperly term'd for the Smell being so very strong and offensive that I could not force my horse Near the Well ... the taste and smell is much of Sulpher' tho' it has an additionall offenciveness Like Carrion.. I drank a quart in a morning for two days and hold them to be a good sort of Purge if you can hold your breathe so as to drink them down.

Daniel Defoe

Defoe in his *Tour Through the Whole Island of Great Britain* had something of a jaundiced view in 1717:

We were surprised to find a great deal of good company here ... though this seems to be the most desolate and out-of-the-world place, and that men would only retire to it for religious mortifications, and to hate the world, but we found it quite otherwise.

Henry Smollett

Henry Smollett's baleful description of his Harrogate spa experience in Humphrey Clinker:

At night I was conducted into a dark hole on the ground floor, where the tub smoked and stunk like 'the pit of Acheron'. Acheron is a name for the river that runs through Hell. After staying in the town in 1766 Smollett describes Harrogate as 'a wild common, bare and bleak, without tree or shrub or the least signs of cultivation'.

Thorpe's Illustrated Guide of 1886 gives us another list of conditions for which the sulphur waters provide effective therapy: 'pimples which rise with great itching, ulcerated tetters, scorbutic rash, shingles, leprosies, branny scales, scaly tetter, grog blossoms produced by intemperance.'

Charles Dickens

Charles Dickens visited the Spa Rooms to deliver some readings in 1858 and said, 'Harrogate is the queerest place with the strangest people in it, leading the oddest lives of dancing, newspaper reading and tables d'hote.'

Despite this, numbers of drinkers continued to rise from 3,774 in 1842, 11,626 in 1867 and 259,000 in 1925.

3. The Harrogate Hotels – Behind Closed Doors

St George Hotel

The St George Hotel, opposite the Kursaal, developed slowly but surely from its origins as a small cottage. From 1778 it began to offer the services of an inn. On 9 May 1910 Princess Victoria, the king's sister, and the Grand Duchess George of Russia, watched from a window there the proclamation of George V as king and emperor on the steps of the Royal Baths.

Other 1930s Harrogate accommodation included the Harrogate Food Reform Guest House in St Ronan's Road, where 'dieting is understood'; on the other hand Miss Hamilton at the Octagon Boarding House ensures a 'liberal table'.

The Swan

The Swan Inn was built around 1700 as the Old Swan and run by Jonathan Shutt who began receiving visitors at 'the Sign of the Swan'; in 1820 it was rebuilt and named the Harrogate Hydropathic, reverting first to the Swan Hydropathic and then to the Swan Hotel in 1953. The Hydropathic was the first in Harrogate to be lit by electricity. The first resident physician (and one of the directors) was a Dr Richard Veale who came from Cornwall to Harrogate to develop hydropathic cures; it was originally modelled on Smedley's Hydro at Matlock. To make it fully compliant with its health objectives, the Hydro sacrificed its alcohol license, banned smoking and made morning prayers compulsory. Visitors must have enjoyed something of a monastic stay.

The Harrogate Hydropathic had 200 bedrooms, a dining room for 300 'patients', in addition to the coal fires, hot and cold running water. Bathing at the hotel was only available in the new suite of medicinal baths. Toilets had extractor fans to combat sulphured hydrogen fumes. Dr Veale instigated strict regimes, including control over diet, baths, exercise, massage and careful water drinking.

The famous swan sign was made to commemorate the coronation of Queen Elizabeth II in 1953. The Beatles apparently stayed here during their 1963 visit for the concert at the Royal Hall; General Manager Geoffrey Wright was appalled at the idea of them darkening his portals but took their money anyway. The group had tried to get into the Hotel St George, but were turned away because their appearance was deemed inappropriate.

Harrogate had not always enjoyed clean living and the high life. In 1821 the people of Harrogate had complained to the council about sporadic vandalism: 'during the night some persons unknown ... have put into the mineral springs some quantities of Dung, Ashes, Dead Dogs, and other animals of a most offensive nature.' In 1841 the Harrogate Improvement Act was passed to protect the springs.

In 1926 Agatha Christie took refuge here (when it was The Harrogate Hydro).

A week's stay in 1926 cost £5 10s. A 1948 advert lists the facilities, which included 'commodious and artistically appointed' public rooms;

A first-class Orchestra plays daily in the Lounge, and the Saturday evening Dinner Dances are a feature of Yorkshire Social Life. There are two Championship Squash Courts ... Tennis Courts and Putting Greens are available in the grounds ... special diets for visitors taking the cure are a feature of the hotel.

Guests included Edward Elgar in 1927 who tetchily declared 'Harrogate thinks of itself very fashionable and more than a little chic, and the ladies dress up terribly.'

The Old Swan Hotel hosted the International Toy Fair for the town in the 1960s, thus paving the way for Harrogate to become a leading conference and fair venue.

Agatha Christie and The Swan

The year 1926 was not a good one for Mrs Christie: her mother had passed away earlier that year and she discovered that her husband was having an affair. She had left her home in Sunningdale, Berkshire about 9.45 p.m. on 3 December, abandoned her car leaving it perched precariously on the edge of a chalk pit called Silent Pool at Newland's Corner in Surrey, and caught a train to Harrogate after seeing a random railway poster advertising the resort. She may have been suffering from amnesia, possibly brought on by a nervous breakdown. At the time, however, popular opinion, ever cynical, had it that Christie had merely staged a publicity stunt to boost her book sales.

She checked in under the name of Theresa Neele, bizarrely, the name of her husband's mistress, and set about enjoying her stay – so began the hotel's association with murder, mystery and suspense.

Meanwhile, a nationwide search was underway – the first in the country to involve aeroplanes and the biggest then in British history. After ten days Bob Tappin, a banjo player at the hotel, recognised Mrs Christie, alerted the police, and so drew a close to this particular mystery. In 1979, *Agatha* the film was released starring Vanessa Redgrave, Dustin Hoffman and Timothy Dalton; some of which was shot in The Swan and in the vicinity of the hotel.

In 2006, then Doctor Who producer Phil Collinson realised a personal ambition. He confided to executive producer Russell T. Davies that he had always wanted to screen an adventure in which the Doctor would encounter Agatha Christie. Gareth Roberts was to be the scriptwriter. Doctor Who, of course, would not be Doctor Who without a monster: Roberts recalled a cover illustration for Christie's *Death In The Clouds* (published in 1935) which depicted a biplane being attacked by a giant wasp. Roberts developed this into the Vespiform: the title of the episode became The Unicorn and the Wasp. The board game, Cluedo, had a part to play: six of the chief suspects corresponded to the six characters of the board game – Colonel Mustard (Colonel Curbishley), Professor Plum (Professor Peach), Reverend Green (Reverend Golightly), Miss Scarlett (Miss Redmond), Mrs Peacock (Lady Eddison), and Mrs White (Miss Chandrakala) – and many of the game's weapons and locations were echoed in the script.

The Crown

Built originally in 1740 by Joseph Thackwray, great uncle of the owner of Montpellier Square and Gardens, it was renovated in 1847 and again in 1870. Thackwray was given permission to buy the Crown Hotel by King George III in 1778. In 1784 the head waiter, William Thackwray was making so much money that he was able to buy the Queen Hotel. Thackwray was no fool: as noted, in 1822 he discovered a number of new wells, one of which was a sulphur well called the Crown Well and another he channelled into the back yard of the Crown. This led to an Act of Parliament giving Harrogate powers to protect their mineral waters against such piracy.

Lord Byron stayed in 1806 with 'a string of horses, dogs and mistresses'. While here he wrote 'To a Beautiful Quaker', inspired it seems when he happened to notice a pretty Quaker girl nearby. The first stanza of the poem is taken from the first edition of *Fugitive Pieces* published in 1806:

> Sweet girl! Though only once we met,
> That meeting I shall ne'er forget;
> And though we ne'er may meet again,
> Remembrance will thy form retain.
> I would not say, 'I love', but still
> My senses struggle with my will:
> In vain, to drive thee from my breast,
> My thoughts are more and more represt;
> In vain I check the rising sighs,
> Another to the last replies:
> Perhaps this is not love, but yet
> Our meeting I can ne'er forget.

An 1865 Meet outside the Crown Hotel.

Elgar visited in 1912. In the Second World War the government requisitioned the Crown for the Air Ministry – they finally vacated in 1959.

White Hart Hotel
Built in 1846 this neoclassical building is, in Pevsner's estimation, 'easily the best building in Harrogate ... with nothing gaudy or showy about it'. The Jarrow Crusaders paused here on The Stray to the front of the hotel in 1936 en route to London.

The Granby Hotel
Harrogate's reputation for fine hotels grew from a need to accommodate the increasing numbers of visitors to what was quickly becoming one of Europe's finest spas. Former

Looking down to the White Hart hotel, with the Victoria Inn (now demolished) at the bottom of Cold Bath Road in 1890.

names of the Granby include The Sinking Ship (not bad branding but a reference to the defeat of the Spanish Armada) and The Royal Oak – Royal Oak was its name when Blind Jack of Knaresborough played his fiddle there and Harrogate's first theatrical productions were held in the barn. It was renamed The Granby in 1795. Blind Jack allegedly eloped with the landlord's daughter on the eve of her wedding to another man in the 1830s. Guests have included Lawrence Sterne and Robert, Clive of India. The Granby is now Granby Court Care Home.

The Dragon Hotel

First records of the Dragon (named after a racehorse of Charles II) go back to 1764 when the owners, the Liddals, won the famous Dunmow Fitch; this entailed married couples going to Dunmow, Essex, and swearing that for a year and a day they had never had a quarrel and never wished themselves not married. The hotel was also called the Green Dragon and was owned between 1827 and 1830 by Thomas Frith, father of the painter W. P. Frith. In 1870 it became High Harrogate College and was demolished in the 1880s to make way for Mornington Crescent.

Many of the hotels in Harrogate grew out of farmhouses: the popularity of the town as a spa rather took it by surprise and many visitors were initially accommodated in extended farmhouses with meals comprising produce from the farms. The Dragon, Granby and Queen all were originally farms.

The Queen Hotel

The hotels soon acquired nicknames, indicative of their clientele. The Granby, popular with the aristocracy, was known as 'The House of Lords'; The Dragon was 'The House of Commons' due to its patronage by the military and the racier set; The Crown was known

The Dragon hotel; formerly the Green Dragon.

as 'The Hospital' because it was close to the Old Sulphur Well. The Queen was frequented by tradesmen and merchants and was known as 'The Manchester Warehouse'. It was probably named after Charles II's wife, Catherine of Braganza; now The Cedar Court, it was reputedly Harrogate's first-purpose built hotel. Blind Jack was resident fiddler here around 1732. Like The Grand, The Queen was requisitioned by the Empire Pilot's Receiving Scheme during the Second World War. It became the headquarters for the regional health authority in 1950 but happily reverted to its intended use in 1990.

Hotel Majestic

The Majestic's origins lie in a dispute between a local businessman, Sir Blundell Maple, and the Queen Hotel. On checking his bill one morning at The Queen, Sir Blundell spotted an error; not receiving satisfaction from the Queen's manager he stormed out threatening to build a hotel which would put The Queen out of business. And so was born the Majestic – fine hotel as it was and is – it nevertheless failed to ruin The Queen. Guests have included Elgar, Winston Churchill, Errol Flynn and George Bernard Shaw.

Thomas Baskerville (died 1840), surgeon and botanist, speaks plainly of his irritation at the over-eager water servants invading even The Queen's hotel rooms to ladle out the water: guests were met with "'I am pretty Betty, let me serve you" … "Kate and Cozen Doll, do let we tend you" … but to tell the truth they fell short of that for their faces shone like bacon rine. And for beauty may view with an old Bath guide's ass.'

The hotel was badly damaged by fire in 1924 causing £50,000 worth of damage. It also has the dubious distinction of being on the wrong end of one of three bombs Harrogate received during the Second World War. The hotel was listed as a target for German

20 June 1924: the day the Majestic went up in flames.

The German–British motor toured of 1911 passing the front of The Majestic. Prince Henry of Prussia was a competitor.

bombers in 1940 because German intelligence wrongly had it down as housing the Air Ministry. Indeed, Harrogate was second in the list of priority targets which includes Hughendon Manor at the top (headquarters of Fighter Command); various garrisons, the headquarters of Bomber Command, the Admiralty and other sensitive installations. In the event a Junkers 88 dropped three bombs at midday on 12 September 1940: one exploded in the hotel gardens, one on the corner of Swan and Ripon Roads demolishing a house, and the other hit The Majestic but failed to explode. This was rendered safe by a Captain G. H. Yates of the bomb disposal squad.

The Cairn Hydro

Built in 1890, the hotel was renamed the Cairn Hotel. In 1896 £2.09s to £3.10s got you a bed, attendance, table d'hote, breakfast, luncheon, afternoon tea, a free bath every morning and a copy of the *Cairn Times*. Evidence that the very early inns or hotels were somewhat low-rent comes from Lady Verney in a letter of 1665:

> We arrived att the nasty Spaw, and have now began to drinke the horrid sulphur watter, which allthowgh as bad as is poasable to be immajaned, yet in my judgement plesent to all the doings we have within doorse. The House and all that is in it being horridly nasty, and crowded up with all sorts of company, which we eate with in a roome, as the spiders are ready to drop into my mouth, and it sure hathe nethor been well cleaned nor ared this dousen years; it makes me much more sicke than the nasty watter.

Unlikely that she ever went back ...

The Grand Hotel

Opened in 1903 on Cornwall Road opposite the Sun Pavilion, the former grand Grand Hotel is now Windsor House and home to offices. During the First World War it was converted into the Furness Military Hospital. In common with other hotels in the town, it was requisitioned by the Ministry of Defence during the Second World War, too, for the Empire Pilot's Receiving Scheme; unfortunately it struggled to re-establish itself as a hotel post-war. The lounge was famous for its tapestries depicting old Harrogate and murals illustrating English spas. Conri-Tait and his band were the resident entertainment in the 1930s.

The Prospect Hotel

Originally a private house built in 1814 by Nicholas Carter Snr, it gradually developed into a hotel as the owner took on more and more guests during the season. After a series of reconstructions the hotel, then named the Prospect, had doubled in size by 1870 and sported its eighty-two-foot tower. The fine ironwork on the façade was removed in 1936. Today it is the Yorkshire Hotel.

Before the age of the bath chair, transportation was more basic: in 1660 the local constable claimed 7d for 'carrying one cripple to Harrogait on horseback'. In 1810 a journalist by the name of Henry Curling had waxed lyrical about the town:

> What scenes of life have we not beheld at Harrowgate. What days of romance and nights of revelry and excitement have we not passed...where mothers trotted out their daughters in all their charms and country squires learnt the trick of wiving.

A bath chair rank outside the Prospect Hotel. 1s 3d for the first hour – 4d for every extra fifteen minutes.

The Prospect Hotel dominates.

Some fine-looking 1930s automobiles in Prospect Gardens.

4. Harrogate Social Life

Inside the Blues Bar in Montpellier.

Taking the waters is one thing, but what do you do with all that gentry and nouveau riche, with its disposable income, once they have completed their daily cleansing, inside and out? Local hoteliers soon realised that their guests needed somewhere to go for special occasions and evening entertainment – entertainment being just as critical a remedy for the ill and infirm as spa treatments. Things became more critical when what was seen as the lower orders piled in on the newly developed railways.

In 1788 the only entertainment there was in Harrogate was provided by hotels like the Crown, which engaged strolling players to entertain the gentry up to eighty persons at a time.

John Feltham's 1804 *Guide to All the Watering and Sea-Bathing* tells us how Harrogate society worked and notes the practice of men and women remaining in the same room after dinner whereby 'the ladies, by this custom, have an opportunity of witnessing the behaviour of gentlemen; and the latter of determining how well qualified the former may be for presiding over a family.' On entertainment generally:

> Deep play, of any kind, is seldom practiced at Harrowgate; the person who could renounce female society, which is here to be had without difficulty, for a pack of cards, or a faro bank, would be generally avoided. Another advantage of mixing freely with the ladies, is the sobriety it ensures; to which the waters, indeed, contribute not a little.

Later, a consortium decided that a larger multipurpose venue with hall and park based on the German *kursaal* (a 'cure' hall for mental refreshment) was needed. Hence, the Harrogate Kursaal was born in 1903, sponsored by Samson Fox and recognised as one of Frank Matcham's fines buildings. Cinematographic shows were held there until the mid-1930s.

Touring companies such as the Carl Rosa Opera Company played; in 1904 they presented a Wagner season. Up to 1930 the hall boasted a fifty-player orchestra; Claude Verity presented his new talking film here in 1921, long before the famous Vitaphone's version.

The Barn and the Regency Theatre

The 1788 theatre had close associations with actor-manager Samuel Butler's Georgian Theatre in Richmond and shared actors and productions with his other theatres in Beverley, Kendal, Northallerton, Ripon, Ulverston and Whitby. The owner of the Granby Hotel in 1788, Mrs Wilks, built the theatre in Church Square; before this it was in the barn at the Granby – a common situation for theatres in England at the time and gives rise to the word 'barnstormers'. Hollins's *1858 Illustrated Handbook* tells us about the barn 'and there it was that the celebrated Miss Melon used to delight her audience, and where her genius shone forth in a blaze of triumph, which completely obscured the light of twelve penny candles flickering in bottles around her'. In the eighteenth century Harrogate people were not used to going out to the theatre: the opening performance attracted an audience of one. The theatre closed in 1830 and became a private house (Mansfield House), as it remains today.

Town Hall Theatre

In Swan Road, this opened in the mid-nineteenth century and was converted into a theatre in 1882. D'Oyley Carte performed there in Gilbert and Sullivan's *Patience* in 1883; as did Lilly Langtry in 1885's *Peril.* It closed as a theatre soon after in the late 1890s.

Pavilion Theatre

A travelling theatre which performed in the very early twentieth century where a railway goods yard now stands. The theatre also took in such towns as Wetherby, Tadcaster, Malton, Bedale and Bridlington.

Promenade Rooms

The Promenade Rooms were originally built in 1805 and rebuilt by Arthur Hiscoe in 1875. It is now the Mercer Art Gallery, home to Harrogate's fine art collection. The building was paid for by public subscription and was used as a meeting place for people to make 'polite conversation' after taking the waters. It was also used as a theatre, where, in 1884, Lilli Langtry (mistress of Edward VII) performed *School for Scandal*. Oscar Wilde also gave an address on dress here.

Cheltenham Spa Rooms

A magnificent classical building, built in 1835 with superb Doric columns, was constructed to complement the Cheltenham Spring, so-called because the waters were considered similar to those in Cheltenham. This had been discovered in 1818 and was soon regarded as the best chloride of iron spring in Europe. Increasing demand led to the building of a new pump room in 1871 by Bown in the style of a miniature Crystal Palace. The building later became known as the Royal Spa Concert Rooms. 6 acres of gardens featured a boating lake and skating rink with a pump room and colonnade built in 1870. These rooms were used for promenading and drinking water from the iron spring on site. A vandalistic corporation bought the rooms in 1896 and demolished the lot in 1939. The pillars survive though, and can be seen at RHS Harlow Carr.

The Grand Opera House

The Grand Opera House opened in 1900 in Oxford Street, the premiere was a charity gala, *The Gentlemen in Khaki*, in aid of British soldiers fighting the Boer War; next on was a run of 'Dick Whittington'. Designed by Frank Tugwell, who also designed the Futurist Theatre in Scarborough and the Savoy Theatre in London, the Opera House incorporated many of the latest safety features of the day: a fireproof curtain which could be lowered between the stage and the auditorium; fire extinguishers and a sprinkler system; hot and cold running water in the dressing rooms and electric lighting. In 1933 the Opera House became a repertory theatre. The original capacity was 1,300, later reducing to 800. In 1958 the theatre reopened as Harrogate Theatre, and in the early 1970s was extensively refurbished with capacity further reducing from to 480. Over the years many famous

Part of the splendid restoration of Harrogate Theatre.

performers have appeared at Harrogate, including the d'Oyley Carte Company Trevor Howard, Charlie Chaplin and Sarah Bernhardt.

St James' Picture House

Opened in Cambridge Street in the early 1900s. An incredulous review in 1907 described 'remarkable displays of animated pictures ... not the least attractive part of the show is the realistic way in which the pictures are made to speak'. From 1882 it was the club room for the Conservative Club and Public Coffee House Ltd. The picture house closed in 1960 and gave way to yet another supermarket.

The Empire Theatre

Opened in 1910 in Cheltenham Mount as a conversion from an 1872-built church. It had a reputation for bawdy entertainment. It closed in the late '20s reopening as the Gaiety, 'the cosiest theatre in the north'.

Palace Theatre

Palace Theatre on Skipton Road opened in 1914 and changed its name to the Ritz in 1947. It closed in 1962 in submission to bingo.

Central Cinema

This cinema opened in 1920 in Oxford Street and closed in 1949. It was demolished in 1961 and a supermarket is now on the site.

The Odeon

East Parade (not 'Oscar Deutch Entertains Our Nation' – just the ancient Greek name for a theatre). The Odeon in Harrogate is one of the few remaining custom-built Odeons. Designed by Harry Weedon and built in 1936 at a cost of £50,000, the cinema opened with the showing of *Where's Sally?* and *Carry on Matron*.

Regal

Built in 1937 on the site of St Peter's schoolrooms on Cambridge Road. In 1973 it underwent a conversion with the circle left as a cinema (494 seats) while the stalls became a pub-cum-mini-cinema with 180 seats.

The Kursaal

Modelled loosely on the resplendent Ostende Kursaal in Belgium, it was opened in May 1903 by Sir Hubert Parry (of *Jerusalem* and *I Was Glad fame*) on the site of Bown's 1870 Cheltenham Pump Room.

Early attractions included Sarah Bernhardt, the Halle Orchestra, Pavlova and Dame Nellie Melba. The name Kursaal (cure hall) comes from the buildings so named and popular in continental spa towns. In Harrogate the name was changed in 1918 to the less Germanic Royal Hall and boasted 1,276 seats. The Kursaal came about as a response to the growing demand for entertainment in Harrogate and because, at the time, the popularity of chloride of water was declining. The Cheltenham Pump Room was demolished to make way for it.

The beautiful Kursaal at Ostende, on which Harrogate's was modelled.

The interior of the Kursaal – opened in 1903 and later renamed The Royal Hall for less Teutonic overtones.

The Royal Hall

The breathtakingly beautiful Royal Hall is now an integral part of Harrogate International Conference Centre which opened in 1981 – the result of a determination in the 1960s to keep Harrogate on the world stage, and thus ensure its economic prosperity. By using the buildings and services which had served the town admirably as a spa, Harrogate turned into a conference and exhibition venue of considerable importance. In 1959 a temporary hall was set up in the Spa Rooms and Gardens and the town was able to accommodate the prestigious Toy Fair a few years later. Today over 2,000 events take place in the centre each year, bringing in nearly £200 million.

There is more gold leaf here than in any other similar auditorium in Britain. In earlier years royal visitors were commonplace, so to speak; on one day in 1911 three queens were in town: Queen Amelia of Portugal, Empress Marie of Russia and Queen Alexandra (Edward VII's widow). Other pre-war royalty included Princess Victoria, King Manuel of Portugal, Prince Henry of Prussia (the Kaiser's brother) and Prince Christopher of Greece. Performers at the Kursaal have included Parry, Elgar, Vaughan Williams, Stanford, Laurel & Hardy, Paul Robeson and Gracie Fields. The Beatles also played here on 8 March 1963.

The equally magnificent interior photographs of the Royal Hall – one set out for a play, the other for full orchestra.

Less savoury visitors included Sir Oswald Mosley, who spoke at a sold-out 1935 Royal Hall rally, and William Joyce – hanged in 1946 for his 'Lord Haw Haw' pro-Nazi broadcasts – made many British Union of Fascists fundraising trips to the town.

Winter Gardens

In the 1930s, the Municipal Orchestra played every morning throughout the year, with free admission for the patients of the baths. Today Wetherspoon runs the establishment but the days of such top-class entertainment by the likes of Britten, Segovia, du Pré and Menuhin are over.

A concert in full swing in the Winter Gardens in the 1920s, possibly Cecil Moon's Palm Court Trio. Popular it certainly was with standing room only; however, not everyone was transfixed: take a look at the two ladies and gentleman at the front on the left ensconced in their newspapers and book; likewise those on the right behind the pianist.

Harrogate Bands

There was always a lot of relaxing and 'listening to the band'. Bands, therefore, were crucial to the social life of the spa. In 1888 it was decided to form a subscription band in Harrogate. Subscriptions duly flowed in and J. Sidney Jones, bandmaster of the Leeds Rifles, was appointed as conductor. The band was always busy: every morning at 7.30 a.m. a performance was given to encourage the ailing to take the 'waters'. More performances followed throughout the morning and afternoon. Tall hats were de rigueur for the bandsmen in their four performances a day – for which they received less than £1 a week. The Harrogate Band website gives us an insight into just how hectic things were for Harrogate bands: http://www.harrogateband.org/.

In 1908, the Harrogate Temperance Prize Band reported expenditure of £108 2s 9d and income of £97 10s 10d, which included the purchase of a new set of uniforms at £54. During that year the band played at Bilton Grange School Sports, Burton Leonard Friendly Societies' Sunday Parade, Railway Servants' Orphans' Sunday Parade and Meeting, Modern College Sports, Cricket Club Charity Match, Harrogate Agricultural Show, Co-operative Society's Children's Gala, Roundhill Sports, Kirkby Overblow Horticultural Show, Primitive Methodist Sunday Meeting in the Bogs Field, Friendly Societies' Hospital Sunday, six times at Kursaal, three times for the British Women's Temperance Association, and have given Free Sacred Concerts for Friendly Societies'

Boy band outside Holroyd's the photographers in 1900 on the corner of Chapel and Parliament Street; it later became Buckley's the drapers.

This shot from 1903 shows Otto Schwartz and his seven-piece band playing one of their frequent concerts outside the Prospect Hotel. Schwartz is the one on the left playing the flute. Entertainment of a different sort came in the composition of verses on the town and its visitors; one example describes a Benjamin Blunderhead: 'And that night for the first time I stagger'd to bed, / With more wine on my stomach than sense in my head, / But a dose of the water as soon as t'was day, / Dispers'd all my headache and left me quite gay.'

Council in aid of the Gala Funds for Harrogate Infirmary, Grove Road Brotherhood, Citizen's Temperance League, Harrogate Football Club, Pleasant Saturday Evening Concerts, and alternate Sundays in the Valley Gardens and Bogs Fields.

Harrogate Town AFC

Things (nearly) kicked off in 1914 when a club was formed as Harrogate AFC playing in the Northern League with their home games at the County Ground behind the County Hotel (now the Mujib restaurant). However, the First World War put paid to all that: Harrogate should have been playing at Bishop Auckland on 5 September, but sent a telegram north two hours before kick-off saying they would not be turning up as most of the team had gone to join the army.

When peace came a meeting was held at the Imperial Café (now Bettys) in May 1919 and eventually Harrogate AFC was formed for the 1919/20 season to play in the West Riding League. The first competitive game was at the Starbeck Lane Ground on 30 August 1919 against Horsforth. Entrance was 5*d* into the ground and 1/3*d* in the stand. Harrogate won 1-0. In 1920 Harrogate joined the newly formed Yorkshire League but were forced to l leave their Starbeck Lane Ground for a 6-acre plot of land at the club's present site, then called Wetherby Lane. The first Yorkshire League game at the new ground took place on 28th August 1920 with a 2-1 win against York YMCA. The Sulphur and Blacks, nicknamed 'The Sulphurites', also played friendlies against league opposition including games against Liverpool at Anfield, and another at Sheffield United in front of a crowd of 15,000.

The season 1930/31 was the club's last in the Yorkshire League. The 1931/32 season was spent in the Northern League just before the club disbanded. Esh Winning (a colliery

Harrogate Hornets in training – the Hornets are the cheerleading team of Harrogate Town. Courtesy of Peter Arnett, Official Photographer, Harrogate Town AFC. The Hornets are getting well known; they are part of a council initiative and are run by Joanne Armstrong. They have won several awards in their cheerleading/gymnastics endeavours.

village five miles to the west of Durham City) had to cancel their game at Harrogate, unable to afford to travel down from Durham. Worse still, for the rearranged match they had to organise a jumble sale to raise money for the journey to Harrogate. Later that season they were forced to raffle a chicken to get to Whitby United for another match. A team called Harrogate Hotspurs was formed in 1935 until the outbreak of war, after which Hotspurs played in the West Yorkshire League changing their name to Harrogate Town in 1948.

The 2012/13 season was the team's best ever run in the FA Cup where they beat League Two team Torquay United 1-0 to go beyond the first round for the first time. They then drew with Hastings United in the second round; the replay at Hastings also finished 1-1; Harrogate lost 5-4 on penalties. In 2015, Harrogate Town finished fifteenth with fifty-two points from forty-two games in the Vanarama Conference North.

Hales Bar

Certainly the most historic and oldest pub in Harrogate, Hales Bar is the town's only traditionally gaslit bar. Its origins hail as far back as the earliest days of the town's rise as a leading spa resort and was one of the first inns to cater for spa visitors after sulphur wells were first established in the mid-seventeenth century. Sulphur springs still bubble beneath the cellar and their unique smell occasionally percolates up to the bar area.

The premises were rebuilt around 1827 when it was known as The Promenade Inn. It was enlarged in 1856 and known as Hodgson's until 1882 when William Hales became the landlord and gave his name to the pub.

The main saloon bar preserves the Victorian atmosphere well, with mirrors and other interesting features and fittings from Victorian days, including traditional gas lighting and cigar lighters. Tobias Smollett most certainly drank here when in May 1766 he visited Harrogate in which he set part of his novel *Humphry Clinker*. It was a favourite

The men's toilets in the gaslit seventeenth-century Grade II-listed Hales Bar; Victorian décor abounds.

too of Sir John Barbirolli when the Hallé Orchestra was in town; some interior scenes for 'Chariots of Fire' were set here.

Royal Baths Chinese Restaurant

The restoration of the Royal Baths is not just about maintaining the magnificent Turkish Baths and Health Spa. There is also the equally magnificent £1.5 million restoration of the Grand Pump Room into a Chinese restaurant. York has its beautiful Assembly Rooms conversion into a grand Italian restaurant; Harrogate has this wonderful restoration. The Pump Room was originally used to dispense the famous mineral waters from a great octagonal mahogany counter, but the real glory of the 1897 building was the famous, iconic dome. 'And it was this magnificent architectural feature that meant love at first sight for restaurateur Mr Hak Ng'.

He explains:

The only reason I'm here is because of the dome. Some people win the lottery, I've won this. It's been a lifelong dream. I wouldn't have spent £1.5 million if it hadn't been for the dome. I spent one year in China to prepare myself for this building. I'd never been to China before, although I ran a Chinese restaurant in Bedfordshire where I transformed a Co-op mini market into an award-winning restaurant ... I work from 9 a.m. till 2 a.m. seven days a week and see my wife only occasionally because she runs our Bedfordshire restaurant. I've had to close my coffee shop there to concentrate more resources on the Harrogate venture.

The website tells us how,

Hak spent the time in China sourcing traditional furniture, crockery and wood carvings and six containers of furniture were imported including a sixteen-person table, measuring five metres long which takes pride of place in the private dining area. It took two and half years and £1.5 million to complete the refurbishment because of its listed building status and objections from Harrogate Civic Society.

The entrance to the magnificent Chinese restaurant which is now in the Royal Baths.

Scala Super Cinema

Opened in October 1920 with 1,400 seats – a model of luxury and comfort. The Scala published its own monthly magazine with competitions, previews and editorials. In June 1950 the name was changed to The Gaumont, opening with Betty Grable starring in *The Beautiful Blond from Bashful* and *The Prisoner of Zenda.* It closed in 1958 with Rod Steiger's *Al Capone* and was demolished in 1962 to be replaced by a Littlewood's store.

The Scala Super cinema in Cambridge Street.

5. Brand Harrogate

Buckleys the drapers and Dickinson's the grocer, which became one around 1900, on the corner of Chapel and Parliament Streets.

Royal Parade and chemists, early twentieth century.

The 2,000-seater auditorium at the 1982 Harrogate International Centre.

Harrogate – Twenty-First Century Conference Centre

With the potentially disastrous decline of the spa the town had to reinvent itself: this led to the establishment of an industry based on conferences and exhibitions. Accommodation, ambience and amenities were all more or less already in place. Exhibition halls were constructed and the International Conference Centre opened in 1981 at a cost of £34 million, the third largest fully integrated conference and exhibition centre in the UK, and one of the largest in Europe. Now it contributes over £150 million to the local economy annually and attracts in excess of 350,000 business visitors every year. The 2,000-seat main auditorium hosted the 1982 Eurovision Song Contest. Overall capacity currently stands at 2,000 (auditorium); 1,600 (exhibition halls); 600 (Queen's suite); 1,000 (Royal Hall). It has expanded over the years to include eight exhibition halls with 16,500 square metres (178,000 square feet) of space. Further refurbishment and expansion is planned which will increase the exhibition space by up to 18,500 square metres at an estimated cost of £45 million.

Crimplene, and Others

Former employers have included ICI, with offices and laboratories at Hornbeam Park, the Central Electricity Generating Board (CEGB), and the Milk Marketing Board. ICI Fibres Laboratory at Hornbeam Park invented Crimplene in the 1950s, named after the Crimple Valley and Beck nearby. Crimplene was largely popular because of its convenient 'wash-and-wear' properties and was often used to make the A-line dress in the 1960s. Similarly, it was popular amongst Mods who liked it for their garish button-down shirts. Crimplene suits were dubbed 'working-men's going-out clothes'.

Bettys

Perhaps the best of all British tearooms are the six exquisite Bettys which thrive in four towns in Yorkshire: two in historic York (St Helen's Square and Stonegate); two in Harrogate (Parliament Street and Harlow Carr); Georgian Northallerton and beautiful Ilkley. Over a million customers pass through these six doors every year.

The story of Bettys begins in September 1907 when a twenty-two-year-old Fritz Butzer arrived in England from Switzerland with no English and no idea of how to reach a town that sounded vaguely like 'Bratwurst', where a job awaited him. Fritz eventually landed up in Bradford and found work with a Swiss confectioners called Bonnet & Sons at No. 44 Darley Street. Whether Bradford was the original objective, and whether Bonnet's was the intended employer is doubtful; in any event they paid him the equivalent of 120 Swiss francs per month with free board. Cashing in on the fashionability of all things French, Fritz changed his name to Frederick Belmont.

Frederick opened his first business in July 1919: a cafe in Cambridge Crescent on three floors fitted out to the highest standards 'furnished in grey, with muted pink panels with old-silver borders [and] candleholders'. The china was grey-blue; the coffee and teapots heavy nickel silver. Day one takings were £30, with £220 for the first week. In 1920 he opened a second cafe and takings for the year were £17,000; customers included Lady Haigh, Lord Jellicoe, the Duke of Athlone and Princess Victoria.

A bakery was built in Starbeck in 1922 followed by tea rooms in Bradford (in the premises of Bonnets, his first employers) in 1924, and Leeds in 1930. York opened on 1 June 1937: 'I acquired premises in York, excellent site, best in York for £25,750, Frederick tells us in his diary. York, of course, featured the famous Belmont Room based on the First Class saloon on the *Queen Mary* on whose maiden voyage Frederick and his wife Claire had sailed the previous year.

Staff from Harrogate, Starbeck, Leeds and Bradford congregating outside the original Bettys in Harrogate just before the 1931 outing to Windermere. Five charabancs carried the 120 or so staff to the Lake District. Owner Frederick Belmont can be seen at the front in the middle. Courtesy of Bettys & Taylors.

Alleged health benefits were a factor in the expansion of sales of milk chocolate in the early twentieth century, aided by claims of high nutritional values afforded by rich, pure milk content. This of course chimed with the traditional claims surrounding so-called medicinal confectionary: lozenges, voice ju-jubes and barley sugar for example all claimed medical benefits as indeed did Mackintosh's toffee – good for sore throats. Bettys, who produced their own chocolate for sale in their York and Harrogate cafes, tell us that sound German medical research proves that eating chocolate leads to weight loss and is beneficial in the fight against heart disease. Chocolate manufacturers' posters and advertisements of the day were populated with healthy, rubescent children and shapely women.

The true identity of Betty has never been revealed and almost certainly never will be. Speculation is rife, however, and there have been many claimants. She may have been the daughter of a doctor who practiced next door to the cafe and who died from tuberculosis; she could have been Betty Lupton, Queen of the Harrogate Wells from 1778–1838 and chief 'nymph'; she might also have been the actress Betty Fairfax who starred in the West End musical 'Betty' around 1915 and to whom Frederick took something of a shine; moreover, the musical toured the country and came to Harrogate's Grand Opera House three times between 1916 and 1918. Or, just as plausibly, Betty may be the name of the little girl who brought in a toy tea tray during a meeting at which the name for the new cafe was being discussed ...

During the Second World War Bettys stayed open and, like other cafes and restaurants, proved resourceful in making a little go a long way. Powdered egg, utility flour, corned beef, spaghetti and beans and all manner of scraps were put to good use. On one occasion Frederick bought a lorry load of honey salvaged from a bombed warehouse and made fudge from it – a rare delicacy in wartime. Occasionally, war brides were unable cut their cakes as the cake was nothing more than an iced-over cardboard box.

There are 250 staff at Bettys & Taylors handling 200,000 sacks, barrels and chests of tea every year: they buy, taste, roast pack and ship Yorkshire Tea and other special blends. They import from Sri Lanka to Japan, from Java to Ethiopia – twenty-one countries in all, in three continents; the seven buyers between them travel to all of these; the tasters, or blenders, taste up to 300 teas everyday – they take five years to train and spend eighteen months abroad: six months each in Kenya and India and Sri Lanka, and six months in China. Bettys & Taylors work with the changing seasons in each of the countries because the seasons affect the crop and the taste of the tea; they work with climate change because rainfall, rainy seasons and sunshine patterns fluctuate, and so does the taste of the tea. The Tropical House there is full of tea, coffee and cocoa plants – a micro-environment for Yorkshire Tea and the specialty teas from around the world.

It was Bettys & Taylors who bought the very last lot of tea at the London Tea Auction before its closure on 29 June 1998: a 44-kilo chest of Ceylon Flowery Oekoe. Taylors fought off competition from Twinings, paying £555 per kilo for the lot. The money went to charity; needless to say, it was the highest amount ever paid.

Taylors of Harrogate and Yorkshire Tea

The famous tea house, run by Taylors, was in Valley Gardens. Taylors also handled the catering at the Winter Gardens and at the Royal Spa Concert Rooms.

Taylors of Harrogate has its origins during the reign of Victoria when in 1886, Quaker Charles Edward Taylor and his brother Llewellyn – sons of a York pea-dealer and master grocer – set up the tea and coffee importing business C. E. Taylor & Co. Both brothers were apprenticed at the famous Ashby's Tea of London, where they also went on to buy their teas and coffees at auction. Llewellyn eventually took a back seat but Charles soon opened up 'kiosk' tea and coffee-tasting rooms in the popular, fashionable spa towns of Harrogate (at No. 11 Parliament Street) and Ilkley. The kiosks were followed by Café Imperials in both towns: Ilkley opened in 1896; the Harrogate branch in 1905 in the mock Scottish castle now occupied by Bettys. The Ilkley Bettys is the old Taylors 'kiosk' café and Bettys in York's Stonegate occupies the former Taylors 'kiosk' cafe.

His time at Ashbys taught Taylor just how crucial the local water was to particular blends of tea. Local guesthouse owners and hoteliers would come to select blends of tea that Charles had formulated to suit their local water. Today, 'Yorkshire Tea for Hard Water' is blended to give people in hard water areas a proper brew that's bright, brisk and

Above: The tea house in Valley Gardens; note the sun shades in the foreground.

Left: Tea testing at Taylors: veteran tea-taster and Taylors' last chairman, James Raleigh (1907–1999). (Courtesy of Bettys & Taylors)

strong – a skill passed down through generations of Taylors tea blenders and who are the only British blender to do this. In 1962 the manager of a rival café, Bettys, apparently overheard two businessmen mention that the Taylor family were putting their business up for sale. She immediately told Victor Wild, Bettys' chairman, who swiftly bought Taylors for the tea and coffee importing, blending and roasting business to complement Bettys' lines and outlets. Taylors' slogan was: 'They came to take our waters; they much prefer our tea'.

Harrogate Spring Water

The first bottles of water in Britain were apparently produced here in 1740, full of Harrogate's special mineral waters. By 1914 they were the world's biggest exporter of bottled water, hydrating, amongst others, troops from India to the western front.

Farrah's

Founded in 1840 by John Farrah, the shop was originally on Royal Parade but closed in the mid-1990s and now stands on Montpellier Parade. The aim of Original Harrogate Toffee was intended to cleanse the palate of the putrid taste of Harrogate's sulphur water. Original Harrogate Toffee is similar to both butterscotch and barley sugar and uses three different types of sugar, butter and lemon to give a unique texture and flavour. It is still made in copper pans and packaged in the recognisable trademark blue and silver embossed tins.

Ogden's

In 1893 James Roberts Ogden opened The Little Diamond Shop in Cambridge Street, the genesis of what was to become one of Britain's most famous and prestigious jewellers. The impressive Edwardian shop front and showrooms in the current James Street shop bought in 1910 still retains many of the original Edwardian features. Down the years Ogden's has supplied jewellery and silverware to royalty and heads of state including Mrs F. D. Roosevelt, George VI and Princess Marina. Sir Winston Churchill had a silver cigar case made by Ogden's. J. R. Ogden was a celebrated Egyptologist and was adviser to Howard Carter and Sir Leonard Wooley. Carter, of course, went on to discover the Tomb of Tutankhamun in 1922. J. R. Ogden was also Advising Goldsmith to the British Museum and was involved in the restoration of some of the most precious gold artefacts found in museums around the world. The company is currently run by the fourth and fifth generations of the family. A branch opened in York in 2015, in Minster Gates.

Ogden's was frequently called upon to take selections of jewellery to guests in their hotels for them to choose their purchases there. It is this which led to the practice of hotels having jewellery display boxes in their public areas. A 1931 advertisement declares Ogden's to be 'uncommonly famous for rare jewels and pearls' and makes much of its prestigious branch in London's Duke Street.

Wilson & Son

Wilson's, at No. 2 James Street, boasted an association with Savory & Moore, New Bond Street, London chemists to Queen Victoria. They were famous for their attractive and imaginative window displays from the early 1900s when windows were crucial to drawing in custom, before the days of in shop point of sale and self-service. Medicated wines, surgical appliances and photographic services were available. An 1886 advertisement tells us that their service has 'all the accuracy, despatch and elegancy of the best houses in London and Paris'. Wilson & Son had another shop in West Park Stray. In 1928 their premises were bought by Ogden's the jewellers, who already owned the premises next door.

J. Baxter in Havana House
Founded in 1868 in Parliament Street. Barling's pipes, Muratti cigarettes and Loewe briar pipes are amongst the wonderful items on display. Muratti was originally a German brand of cigarettes popular worldwide largely because of the famous commercial created by the legendary Oskar Fischinger – an animator, film-maker and abstract painter. Muratti is now part of Phillip Morris Companies Inc. One of Muratti's original brands was 'Young Ladies Cigarettes'. Both B. Barling & Sons and Loewe were kings among pipe makers. Originally eighteenth-century silversmiths, Barling is famous for the fine silver work with which they adorned pipes from 1812; it was Loewe of Haymarket who first introduced briar pipes to English smokers in 1856.

The Charabanc trade
Burgess' Livery Stables and Mackay & Fowler Carriage Manufactory were prominent at the end of the nineteenth century and specialised in Landaus fitted with patent automatic head. After the First World War, Harrogate witnessed a significant change in its clientele. The exclusive, aristocratic visitors of the pre-war period gave way to what was dismissively called the 'charabanc trade' – obviously not so wealthy but well enough heeled all the same. To cater for this new market the Valley Gardens were developed with the Sun Colonnade and Pavilion, and the Royal Baths were extended.

The tennis courts in Valley Gardens.

Charabancs parked up outside Burgess' Livery Stables in White Hart Mews.

More taxis for hire, outside the Royal Hall.

R. W. Slee

In Tower Street, R. W. Slee ran his Practical Bicycle and Tricycle Fitter business, many years before the riders competing in the Tour de France were to speed through the town in 2014. He also specialised in the repair and 're-India-Rubber tiring' of bath chairs as well as knife cleaning and wringing-machine repairs.

On 5 July 2014, Harrogate served as the finish line of the first stage Leeds–Harrogate section of the Tour de France. This came about in part due to the town's special twin relationship since 1952 with Bagnères-de-Luchon, a French spa town and mineral water producer in the Midi-Pyrénées region of south-western France, which is one of the obligatory stages of the French section of the world-famous race.

Daleside Brewery

Established in the mid-1980s by a family with a brewing heritage stretching back more than 600 years, Daleside moved to their present premises in Starbeck in 1992. Beers include the award-winning Morocco Ale, Old Legover, Ripon Jewel, and Monkey Wrench; export markets include USA, Canada, Australia, Denmark, Sweden and Spain. Morocco Ale was chosen as the beer to accompany the lamb main course at the All Party Beer Groups annual dinner at the House of Commons on in July 2015.

Theakston's Old Peculier Crime Novel of the Year Award

A crime-fiction award, sponsored by Theakston's Old Peculier, is awarded annually in July at Harrogate Crime Writing Festival. The winner receives a cash prize and a small

The 2015 Harrogate Crime Writing Festival, courtesy of Helen McGlynn, Literature Festivals Co-ordinator, Harrogate International Festivals, www.harrogateinternational festivals.com.

hand-carved oak beer cask fashioned by one of Britain's last coopers. It is the only such crime-fiction award in the UK to be voted for partly by the public. In 2014 the winner was Belinda Bauer for *Rubbernecker*. The website tells us that for 2015 'The longlist ... sees stalwarts Ian Rankin, Lee Child and John Harvey in the running. Rankin and Child battle it out, each with their nineteenth novels in the iconic Rebus and Reacher series. Lee Child's number one global bestseller *Personal* takes on Rankin's *Saints of the Shadow Bible*, which brought Rebus back from retirement.'

Olympic Fire
The Olympic Cauldron for the 2012 London Olympics was built in a 'Bond Gadget Workshop' in Harrogate, designed by Thomas Heatherwick.

Leeds Bradford International Airport
Ten miles to the south-west of Harrogate, Leeds Bradford International Airport is the UK's highest at 681 feet (208 m) above sea level. By the number of passengers handled in 2014, it was the sixteenth busiest airport in the UK. It is currently a base for Jet2.com, Monarch Airlines and Ryanair. Thomson Airways is seasonally based at the airport.

The airport opened as the 'Leeds and Bradford Municipal Aerodrome', Yeadon Aerodrome, on 17 October 1931 and was operated by the Yorkshire Aeroplane Club on behalf of Leeds and Bradford Corporations. Scheduled flights began in 1935 with a service by North Eastern Airways from London (Heston Aerodrome) to Newcastle upon Tyne (Cramlington), later extended to Edinburgh (Turnhouse). In June 1935, Blackpool and West Coast Air Services started a service to the Isle of Man. By 1936 the London to

Edinburgh service was flying three times a week; it now stopped at Doncaster and carried on to Aberdeen (Dyce). Seasonal flights between Yeadon and Liverpool followed.

During the Second World War civil aviation was suspended, starting in 1939. Avro built a new secret shadow factory, to produce military aircraft, just to the north of the aerodrome; around 5,515 aircraft were produced and delivered from Yeadon including: Anson (over 4,500), Bristol Blenheim (250), Lancaster bomber (695), York (45) and the Lincoln (25). Two new runways, taxiways and extra hangars made Yeadon an important site for military aircraft test flying.

Civil flights resumed after the war: in 1955 flights to Belfast, Jersey, Ostend, Southend, the Isle of Wight and Düsseldorf began with scheduled flights to London in 1960, and Dublin soon after. A new runway was opened in 1965, the same year the terminal building was destroyed by a fire; the replacement terminal opened in 1968.

In 1997 1,254,853 passengers used the airport in 26,123 movements; this had risen to 3,274,474 passengers in 30,663 movements in 2014. In 2013 the top three destinations were Malaga, Palma de Mallorca and Alicante (240,080 passengers, 231,404 and 231,361, showing a 5, 14 and 13 per cent increase respectively over 2011). Since 2000 the airport has been home to the Yorkshire Air Ambulance. Rail and road links to the airport remain appalling and lamentable – stuck, it seems for the foreseeable future, in the 1940s despite lame promises of a 'powerhouse of the north' transforming the region.

The Great Yorkshire Show

Before 1951 when Harrogate became the official home, the Great Yorkshire Show was held in a different town every year. Now, the three-day event attracts over 100,000 visitors onto its 350-acre site and becomes the temporary home for 8,000 animals, including 1,000 horses and ponies. Over 900 stalls and stands offer every kind of product and service imaginable.

The Great Yorkshire Show came into being in October 1837 when a group of leading agriculturalists, led by the third Earl Spencer, met at the Black Swan Hotel in Coney Street, York, to discuss the future of the farming industry. The result was the inauguration of the Yorkshire Agricultural Society – whose aims were to improve and develop agriculture

The Great Yorkshire Show in 1954, the third year of its permanent residency to which 80,508 people flocked to see 335 trade stands 570 horses, 618 cattle, 298 sheep, 530 pigeons, sixty-six beagles and 327 pigs ...

and to hold a prestigious annual show. The first Yorkshire Show was held in Fulford, York, in 1838. The first recorded attendance figures were in 1842 when the show was again held in York, attracting 6,044 visitors.

The 2014 Tour de France – *les faits et les chiffres*

- Harrogate Borough Council appealed for 3,000 knitted bunting jerseys; they got 23,000.
- 70 kilometres of knitted jerseys were sent out to decorate towns and villages.
- Taylors of Harrogate gave away over 5 million tea bags to spectators lined along the UK stages.
- In Ripley, which is styled on an historic French village complete with Hôtel du Ville, a giant tricolour of flowers was being planted on the castle terraces to be visible from the air and the ground.
- Nearby Knaresborough's town centre was filled with over twenty yellow bikes and fourteen *trompe l'oeil* window murals – two of which feature Yorkshire cycling legends Beryl Burton and Brian Robinson.
- 500,000 Tour spectator guides were published, including versions in Dutch, French and German.

J. Brown's, saddlers of Oxford Street in 1902.

Shaftoes, and Mrs Shaftoe at 12 King's Road.

The Enterprise – a jack of all trades in Skipton Road about 1900: photographic studio, ice creams and hot peas on the left.

Mrs Brogden's famous wool shop at the bottom of Valley Drive where the Valley Gardens are now.

6. In & Around Harrogate

High Harrogate

Before 1800 High Harrogate was Harrogate; Low Harrogate (or Sulphur Wells as it was originally called) was only just beginning to show its potential, due largely to the rise of the Old Sulphur Well. But it was to High Harrogate that people initially came, well-accommodated by the Granby, Queen and Dragon hotels. These hotels succeeded the original boarding houses and, before that, farmsteads where early visitors for the cure stayed – with bath tubs and casks of water from the wells brought in by maids. This is how Thorpe described the development of hotel facilities around the waters:

> The few farm houses and cottages constituting Harrogate were besieged by the aristocratic families of the kingdom, who compelled building enterprise, especially as regards inn accommodation. During 1687 the 'Queen's Head' – afterwards the – 'Queen Hotel' – was erected. The 'Royal Oak', now the 'Granby', the 'World's End', now 'Grove House' followed in the same century, and others succeeded later, viz., the historical

Smart-looking coach and
four on The Stray in 1911.

'Crown' and the 'Dragon', the home of Frith, RA, some of whose early efforts, by the way,
are now in the 'Granby Hotel'.

The Stray

The Stray came about after the punitive 1770 Acts of Enclosure with the Duchy of
Lancaster Commissioners' great award of 1778; this ensured that 200 acres of land
linking the wells would remain open, thus protecting public access to the springs and
allowing space for people to exercise in – exercise was just as important a factor in the
cure as the waters. In addition, the land was used for concerts and accommodated a
racecourse for a while from 1793. Eli Hargrove opened a subscription library nearby
around 1775. For Queen Victoria's Jubilee in 1887 a huge barbecue was held on The
Stray; the people of Harrogate roasted an ox for twenty-four hours, ate 4,000 buns and
drank 500 gallons of beer. In the Second World War trenches were dug to prevent enemy
planes from landing there.

Wedderburn House

Wedderburn House looks out onto The Stray and was the home of the MP Alexander
Wedderburn (1733 to 1805). In 1786 he bought land bounded by The Stray and
built Wedderburn House; John Carr of York is said to have been the architect.
Wedderburn was Lord Chancellor of Great Britain from 1793 to 1801 and became Baron
Loughborough and First Earl of Rosslyn. He was a frequent visitor to the spa and built
the first St John's Well Pump Room in 1786.

Harrogate Racecourse

According to Thorpe, in 1793 there was a racecourse in South Park.

Station Square

Much of this was demolished to make way for the Victoria Gardens Centre; the Queen
Victoria Jubilee Monument was erected in 1887 by Mayor Richard Ellis to mark Victoria's
Golden Jubilee. It was all part of the Victoria Park Company scheme to develop a new

town centre linking the two Harrogates with residential and retail streets. The railway arrived in Harrogate in 1848; the new station opened in 1862 bringing trainloads of tourists and thus heralding the start of Harrogate's tourist industry. Not everyone was enthusiastic though, it was thought by some that the trains would bring the 'lower orders' to the town and reduce the milk yield from local cows.

Station Square with some splendid looking motor cars in the '40s.

An earlier view of the Square from 1911 with bicycle and Station Hotel on the left.

The first taxi cabs to be licensed outside the station in 1908.

The Lord Mayor of London's visit in June 1913 with the state coach passing through Station Square with the Tetley's Station Hotel on the right and the London Rubber Co.

The secret Brunswick tunnel and air-raid shelter.

The Harrogate Underground and Air-Raid Shelter

Few people are aware that there is an old railway tunnel and air-raid shelter underneath Harrogate. The tunnel was abandoned 153 years ago while the far end near Leeds Road section was used as an air-raid shelter during the Second World War.

Phill Davison, a member of the Leeds Historical Expedition Society, has meticulously documented Brunswick railway tunnel and air raid shelter. Here is his account of the tunnel's history:

George Hudson and the York and North Midland railway completed the line from Church Fenton in 1848. When it reached the site of what is now Harrogate's Hornbeam Park station, it veered left and then plunged under the 400 yard long Brunswick tunnel, before emerging on what is now the far side of the Leeds Road/Park Drive roundabout. Here the line followed a discreet cutting before reaching Brunswick station, built opposite Trinity church, on Trinity road next to the Stray. The only evidence the station was here these days is a plaque set in stone opposite the church. The station was built here, because it was not allowed to cross the Stray, for fears of noise and smoke polluting the area. However attitudes had changed towards the railway by 1862 when the North Eastern railway arrived in the town and completed the new station where it still stands today. The branch through Brunswick tunnel and the station was then abandoned after only fourteen years in operation. During the Second World War the tunnel was converted into an air raid shelter with steps leading down to it from the Leeds road roundabout area. Workmen constructing the roundabout in the 1960's accidentally dug into the roof of the tunnel not knowing it was there. The air raid shelter was abandoned by 1943. Today the entrance is filled in leaving no trace it was ever there.

http://www.bbc.co.uk/northyorkshire/content/articles/2008/02/07/harrogate_tunnel_feature.shtml

Before the grill was fitted it provided the ultimate adventure for generations of children who were scared witless down there; it was known as 'the darkie'. The air-raid shelter was built with six-foot-high blast walls and wooden benches running along both sides of the tunnel. Traces of electric cabling suggests that there was a light and power supply down there. The portal has two metal grills to allow bats access.

Phil Catford of Subterranea Britannica adds:

The twin track tunnel which follows the line of Langcliffe Avenue has stone built walls with a brick lined roof arch. There are no refuges or air shafts in its 400 yard length ... There are long stalactites hanging from the roof for much of its length with corresponding stalagmites now forming on the floor ... the indentations left by the sleepers can be clearly seen ... The air raid shelter is located at the west end of the tunnel where a 'room' has been created by building two brick walls across the tunnel. These walls are approximately 8-feet high ... a concrete floor has been laid and brick supports for wooden benches can be seen along both tunnel walls. At each corner, the remains of two brick built chemical toilet cubicles can still be seen ... it was the only large public shelter in that part of Harrogate. Harrogate was only bombed once in 1941 and that was in error when one German plane strayed over the town. The shelter was abandoned by 1943 and sealed. In c. 1954 the tunnel was surveyed for possible use by the Ministry of Supply as an engineering works but it was never used for this purpose.

James Street

At the turn of the twentieth century James Street was paved with wooden blocks to reduce traffic (mainly horse-driven) noise. The superb building with the white tiling was Marshall & Snellgrove. Traffic remains a problem.

James Street in the early 1900s with Standings, the coffee shop from 1883, on the corner. The street was named after James Franklin who owned the land on which the street was built (also Franklin Mount and Franklin Road).

The unveiling of the cenotaph on 1 September 1923 by Princess Mary and Viscount Lascelles.

The Cenotaph

Princess Mary and Viscount Lascelles did the honours on a rainy day 1 September 1923 when they unveiled the war memorial. The noble obelisk that is the cenotaph dominates Prospect Place. Nearly 800 dead or missing are remembered.

Montpellier Parade

Much of this was built in the 1860s by Harrogate builder George Dawson adjacent to Thackwray's Montpellier Gardens. Laid out by Thackwray, the gardens became increasingly popular when the Montpellier Baths were built in 1834. They were, however, much diminished by the construction of the Royal Baths and the Montpellier Baths themselves were demolished in 1895. The octagonal stone building which was the gatehouse to the Montpellier estate survives, but the pump room from 1874 was demolished in 1954.

Thackwray built a small hexagonal pump room in the form of a beautiful Chinese temple which became known as the Montpellier Pump Room in 1822 for the Strong Montpellier, or Crown Spring. Electrotherapy, as we have seen, was all the rage: one of the chief suppliers in the 1880s was the Electropathic Establishment in Volta House, Station Parade, later moving to Chapel Street. Mr W. Hardy, consulting electrician, was assisted there by his niece Miss Burras and specialised in electric, magnetic and hydropathic belts, bands and batteries.

The Royal Baths and the Elephant Man

An extension to the Royal Baths was built in 1911 to house the Plombieres Baths, specialising in the treatment of muco-colitis and other gastrointestinal disorders as championed by Sir Frederic Treves, Serjeant Surgeon to Edward VII. Treves carried out the first successful appendectomy in England in 1888 (until then appendicitis carried a high mortality rate) and it was he who befriended Joseph Merrick, the 'Elephant Man' in The Royal London Hospital for four years. *The Elephant Man* was made into a successful film in 1980 based on Treves's last book. John Merrick was described as a delightful man with a unique style of humour; he suffered from a disfiguring physical disability called neurofibromatosis. This disorder is rare (about 1 in 3,000 people) and is characterized by tumours under the skin, around the nerves, and in the bones. With tragic irony, Treves died of peritonitis; Thomas Hardy, a close friend, composed a poem in his honour and recited it at his funeral.

Municipal Buildings with Cupid and Psyche

Converted in 1931 from the Victoria Baths, which were built in 1871 by the Improvement Commissioners. It was around here and in Crescent Gardens that the morning promenade took place from about 6.30 a.m. Smart dress was essential, as was propriety of the first order. The pavements were washed down twice a day – the first before 7.00 a.m., partly to ensure that ladies' long dresses did not get covered in dust. The beautiful statue of Cupid and Psyche was carved by Giavanni Benzoni for the Spa Rooms Gardens around 1870. When these gardens were dug up in 1958 the statue was astonishingly placed in storage and forgotten about until a chance rediscovery some thirty years later.

A busy start to a busy day in Crescent Gardens in 1911 ... and at the pump room at 8.00 a.m. in a painting by Herbert P. Templar, now in the Mercer Gallery.

Crescent Gardens

Originally laid out in 1890 on the site of the Crescent Inn; this was known as the Globe in the early eighteenth century and then the Half Moon around 1783 when the sulphur springs here were discovered.

The Promenade Room

In Swan Road the Promenade, or Victoria Room, a kind of assembly rooms, to some extent marked the ascent of Low Harrogate over High Harrogate. The presence of sulphur springs as well as iron springs in the lower part of town fuelled its popularity and the 1806 construction of the Promenade Room – where visitors could read the papers, listen to music, play cards, converse and attend balls all for 12s a year – signified its status as the place in Harrogate to be. Unfortunately, it turned out to be nothing of the sort and in 1874 became the Town Hall Theatre (Lilly Langtry and Oscar Wilde performed here), from 1912–1921 the Mechano-Therapeutic Department of the Royal Baths, and then the Old Town Hall.

The Mercer Art Gallery

The Mercer Art Gallery now occupies the site and includes works by Turner, Atkinson Grimshaw, Arthur Rackham and William Powell Frith. Frith was born in Aldfield near Ripon in 1819 and is considered to be one of the most influential artists of the Victorian age. His best-known works are *Life at the Seaside*, *Derby Day* and *The Railway Station*, and the famous *Many Happy Returns of the Day, 1856* – a depiction of Frith's own family at his daughter Alice's sixth birthday. His private life was as hectic and colourful as his art, with a wife and a mistress producing nineteen children. He was a close friend of Charles Dickens, whose novels inspired many of Frith's paintings.

Valley Gardens

In 1887 the Valley Gardens were laid out to commemorate the Golden Jubilee of Queen Victoria's reign. Thirty-six springs rise within one acre of the gardens (there are eighty-nine in the town as a whole and each one is chemically different) all pumped down

Valley Gardens in 1916 with uniformed soldier in the foreground.

to the Royal Baths. The gardens were enlarged in 1901 to what is more or less their current layout. The central part was originally called Bog Fields after the boggy area which used to be there. Granville, in *Spas of England*, describes it as 'Deep sulphur wells, two or three pools of water impregnated with tannin and more than one saline chalybeate ... which altogether has the appearance of a great chemical laboratory of nature.'

The metal covers with their unique numbers indicating the presence of a spring or well beneath have long been removed in the interests of the efficiencies required for grass cutting. In September 1934 the first horticultural show was held in the Valley Gardens; the council received a letter from the Royal Horticultural Society congratulating them on their success. During the Second World War iron railings and lamps were removed and some of the ornamental beds were dug for victory.

The main pathway through the gardens to the Magnesia Well is named Elgar Walk and commemorates the many visits Edward Elgar made to the town. On the other side of the gardens is the Sun Colonnade which leads to the Sun Pavilion. Originally opened in 1933, it was refurbished in 1998 and reopened by Queen Elizabeth II. The Boating Lake is still very popular, a place that has changed very little over the intervening seventy years.

Harrogate began to take part in Britain in Bloom in 1963, boosting the horticultural shows staged in the gardens. In the 1980s the Yorkshire Show Ground was established

Sun Walk, Valley Gardens.

Valley Gardens with bandstand and audience.

The pavilion in
the Valley Gardens
in 1958.

on the outskirts of Harrogate and it was decided that the horticultural shows, which had
outgrown the gardens, be moved to the showground site.

Samson Fox Bottles the Sun

Parliament Street was the first street in Britain to be lit by water gas – supplied from
the water gas plant which stood on the site of the Winter Gardens. It was established
by Samson Fox (1838–1903), who held the still unbeaten record of three-time Mayor of
Harrogate, provider of ox roastings, engineer and inventor. People came from all over
Britain to see how 'the Mayor of Harrogate has bottled the sun.' In 1870, Fox perfected the
process of creating water gas, in his basement laboratory at Grove House. After building
a trial plant at his home on Scarborough Road it became the first house in Yorkshire to
have gas lighting and heating. In his late twenties, he was running his own tool-making
business, called the Silver Cross Works. In 1874, he set up the Leeds Forge Company to
produce 'Best Yorkshire' iron for locomotive and marine engine parts.

Fox founded Harrogate's Grove Road School, donated the town's first fire engine,
funded the Royal Hall, and provided affordable social housing. Fox also invented the
corrugated boiler flue and the pressed steel railway bogey; he helped finance the new
premises of the Royal College of Music in London to the tune of £45,000.

Now a multi-millionaire, Samson Fox built himself a fully equipped workshop in the
basement of Grove House, and added the Royal Stables, which included a Turkish bath
for his breeding stock. The stables clock tower, and much of the interior panelling, stained
glass and plasterwork to create new rooms in the house, were all recovered from the
recently demolished Dragon Hotel, formerly over a bridge on the opposite side of Skipton
Road.

Efforts to expand water gas production across the UK were thwarted by the existing
coal gas companies, as well as by an article written by consumer safety champion and
author Jerome K. Jerome. The water gas plant was eventually demolished in 1897 to make
way for the Winter Gardens. His descendants include his great grandson the actor Edward
Fox, and his daughter, the actress Emilia Fox.

Parliament Street with the Café Kiosk on the right and Buckleys the milliners and dress shop.

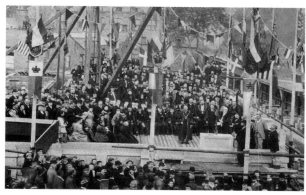

Foundation stone-laying at the Winter Gardens in July 1894.

Grove House

Was built on Skipton Road between 1745 and 1754 as World's End Inn, originally a coaching inn and staging post for passengers and mail from London to York; today it is owned by the Royal Antediluvian Order of Buffaloes. In 1805 it was bought by a Mrs Holland for use as a boarding school. In 1809 it was purchased by Yorkshire-born author Barbara Hofland, who developed it as a ladies' finishing school, a forerunner to what is now Harrogate Ladies' College. The Reverend T. T. Wildsmith bought it in 1822, and converted it into a school for boys, Harrogate College for Boys.

Barbara Hofland wrote some sixty-six didactic moral stories for children, schoolbooks and poetry, most of which describe the struggles of a Christian family against everyday social hardships. She is the author of the long poem: *A Season at Harrogate*, in a series of poetical epistles, from Benjamin Blunderhead Esquire to his mother ... (Knaresborough: R. Wilson, 1812). The opening lines of 'Letter II' give, literally, a flavour:

> Oh! how my dear mother shall pen, ink, and paper
> Convey to your mind a true sense of the vapour,
> Which hov'ring around this new Acheron serves,
> To torture and wound your olfactory nerves,
> And gives you presentiment piercing and strong,
> Of its pungent effects when receiv'd on the tongue.

Of rotten eggs, brimstone, and salts make a hash,
And 'twill form something like this delectable mash
Nothing else in this world I will wager a pasty,
So good in effect, ever tasted so nasty.

During the First World War, Grove House became a convalescence hospital, used for troops from the Battle of the Somme and Battle of Flanders.

Harrogate College for Boys

As was the norm in those days, discipline was taken very seriously; some extracts from the 1893 *Rules for the Boys' College* are very edifying:

> Free conversation is allowed in the dining room but not loud talking or laughter. Reading while eating is forbidden. On leaving the room pupils are expected to bow to the master on duty ... On Sundays no playing or reading unsuitable books is allowed. No talking is allowed going to and from church. All must keep step ... the fine for letting soap, flannel etc choke the bath waste pipe 3*d*; fine for throwing paper on the floor 1/2*d*; fine for losing the copy of the rules 2*d*.

Harrogate Ladies' College

Around the same time there was obvious demand for the boys' sisters and other girls to be similarly educated, and so Mr G. M. Savery, head of the college, opened a small school in Dirton Lodge, Ripon Road, in 1893; tuition fees were £6 per term. The boys' school did not survive and in 1904 the ladies' college moved to the present purpose-built accommodation on the Duchy of Lancaster Estate for eighty boarders and forty day girls. Even in those early days ergonomics was important; L. Ruggles Roberts, writing in the *Girl's Realm* in 1904, tells us 'Here all is charming ... [the desks] are known as Dr Roth's hygienic desks and contain a pad for the support of the pupil's back which may be adjusted to any height ... the desk too may be lifted up or down ... which all prevents the pupil from stooping and becoming round shouldered.' 'Free Lance' in the Harrogate Advertiser adds: 'The rooms are ventilated by air shafts communicating with Boyle's patent Air Pump Ventilators on the roof.'

2 to 4 hours daily were spent in the open air and the gym mistress was trained by the renowned Martina Bergman Osterberg; games included cricket, hockey, vigoro and basket ball. The uniform comprised a green coat and skirt, white blouse and white sailor hat. During the Second World War the school was requisitioned by the MoD and the staff and girls decamped to Swinton Castle, Masham.

Vigoro is a team sport that originally combined elements of cricket and tennis, or baseball. It was invented in 1901 by Englishman John George Grant. Originally, tennis rackets were used and the wicket consisted of six stumps. In 1902, a match was played before the MCC committee at Lord's. They didn't like it, although today it is very popular in Australia. Ashes to ashes ...

Martina Sofia Helena Bergman-Österberg was a well-known Swedish physical education instructor and an important figure in the women's suffrage movement.

She was born in 1849 and died on 29 July 1915. When she moved to London she founded the first physical education instructor's college in England which uniquely only admitted women. Pioneering the teaching of physical education as a subject in its own right within the school curriculum, she also introduced the wearing of gymslips by women playing sports. She also played an influential role in the early development of netball. Martina was extremely supportive towards women's education and emancipation, encouraging women to be active in sport and education.

New College, Harrogate

New College was an independent preparatory school in Harrogate which amalgamated with Ashville College in 1930. It was originally founded as Turton Hall School in 1850 and transferred from Gildersome, south of Leeds, to Harrogate in 1898. Revd John Haslam DD was Proprietor of Turton Hall School from 1873 and when the lease ran out in 1898 he purchased land and built New College in Harrogate for £10,000.

In 1900 the New College estate consisted of 34 acres which included a vegetable garden, a farm, two fives courts; a gymnasium; a workshop, two tennis courts, a cinder court and a bicycle track. The boys' department comprised a large dining hall and assembly room with a raised platform for choir and organ for Divine Service, three class rooms, a school parlour, a library, a music room, laboratory, a bath and dressing room, lavatory, boot and two cloak rooms. The senior dormitory had dressing cubicles as recommended by Dr Clement Dukes in his book on *Health at School*: 'All the rooms were heated with hot water pipes, and ventilated on the most approved principles. Special attention was given to the sanitary arrangements.' After the First World War, New College developed rapidly and from 1919 to 1923 there were more than 100 boys there. Typical school trips

New College Harrogate. The Gymnasium.

H Shaftoe Printer Harrogate

The gym at New College.

included climbing the Matterhorn or flying to Paris, on a Handley Page aircraft, from the airport at Croydon.

Harlow Carr

Is one of four public gardens run by the Royal Horticultural Society, acquired by the merger of the Northern Horticultural Society with the RHS in 2001. It had been the Northern Horticultural Society's trial ground and display garden since 1946, where the suitability of plants for growing in northern climates could be studied and assessed. The society leased 10.5 hectares of mixed woodland, pasture and arable land from Harrogate Corporation and opened the Harlow Carr Botanical Gardens in 1950.

Sulphur springs were discovered on the site in the eighteenth century but there was no development of the spa for over a hundred years. In 1840, the owner of the estate, Henry Wright, cleaned out one of the wells and four years later built a hotel and a bathhouse, charging 2s 6d to bathe in the warm waters. The gardens were laid out around the bathhouse. The hotel was Harrogate Arms, but is now closed. The bathhouse now houses the garden study centre. The six well heads in front of the bathhouse have been capped off but remain beneath the present Limestone Rock Garden.

There used to be bandstand here which held frequent pierrot shows. Although the corporation had bought Harlow Moor in 1898, it could not afford the Carr so this was bought privately for £8,500 by three councillors in 1914, who thus secured the gardens for the town. Harlow Carr features, among many other things, the National Collection of Rhubarb. The six imposing Doric columns were salvaged from the Cheltenham Spa Rooms which were demolished in 1939.

On Harlow Moor suitably hatted.

7. Harrogate & The Military

The Military Spa

During the First World War Harrogate took on a truly patriotic, military support role when it opened its hitherto exclusive and elite doors to wounded servicemen for physical rehabilitation and mental and physical recuperation. A prodigious 100,000 servicemen were treated in 1919 alone (no separate records exist for before that), with 600 injured passing through the various doors each week.

Harrogate, of course, benefitted: it won a reputation for being a centre of excellence for post-traumatic injury assessment and rehabilitation, and it attracted business after the war which otherwise would have gone to Baden Baden, and Spa. Unlike Wells, Bath and Buxton, Harrogate made a profit during the war.

The Grand Duchess George of Russia Hospital

The First World War had a number of other impacts on the town: those accustomed to visiting spas on the continent such as Spa and Baden Baden could obviously not do so and came to spas like Harrogate instead; foreign dignitaries in exile sometimes sought refuge in Britain. One such was the Grand Duchess George of Russia, daughter of King George I of the Hellenes; she had married Grand Duke George Mikhailovitch, cousin of Tsar Nicholas II, who was murdered by the Bolsheviks in 1919. She set up a small hospital in Tewit Well Road to help care for the war wounded and recuperating soldiers, and in 1920 erected a memorial to the soldiers who died in her hospital. Princess Alix of Hesse visited in 1894, granddaughter of Victoria and future wife of Tsar Nicholas II.

RAF Yeadon

All a bit of a bungle. No. 609 (West Riding) Squadron was based here from 10 February 1936 until 27 August 1939 when it was posted to Catterick, not returning again until 1946 with their Mosquito Mk XXX aircraft, something of a problem because the runways were too short to operate these aircraft safely. Safety speed (that which the aircraft needs to be flown and controlled on a single engine) was not reached until overflying central Leeds when taking off in that direction – with obvious drastic consequences should things go wrong on take-off. To add to the problems, the airfield sloped downhill, making it necessary to land at RAF Linton-on-Ouse (20 miles away) when the wind was blowing from the wrong direction. Eventually the Air Ministry re-equipped No. 609 with Spitfire LFXVIs' but the grass airstrip was not ideally suited to Spitfire operations, and so it was decided that No. 609 Squadron should move to the hard runways of RAF Church Fenton in October 1950.

When No. 609 Squadron left for Catterick, Yeadon became a Flying Training School, bomber maintenance unit, and a scatter airfield. In January 1942 it was transferred to the Ministry of Aircraft Production, whereupon Avro built their shadow factory. It was also used by Hawker Aircraft for development work on its Tornado design. Yeadon remained active until 1957, operating Austers, Supermarine Spitfires and De Havilland Mosquitoes. RAF Yeadon finally closed in 1959.

Linton-On-Ouse Airport, Harrogate

This is the official name of RAF Linton-on-Ouse (the IATA code is HRT) although no one ever calls it that any more. It is also known, or has been, as Harrogate Airport when it was just that. Linton is 10 miles north of Harrogate as the crow (or Tucano) flies, and about 16 miles by road.

RAF Linton-on-Ouse opened on 13 May 1937 as a bomber airfield and was the home of No. 4 Group RAF until 1940. At the start of the Second World War, bombers from Linton dropped propaganda leaflets over Germany, soon followed by bombing raids on Norway, the Netherlands, Germany, and Italy. Linton was one of eleven stations allocated to No. 6 Group, Royal Canadian Air Force. No. 6 Group flew 40,822 operational sorties dropping 126,000 tons of ordinance. A total of 814 aircraft and approximately 5,700 airmen did not return from operations while 3,500 of these lost their lives out of total Bomber Command losses of 55,000 men. First sortie was 3/4 January 1943 when six Wellingtons from No. 427 Squadron were sent to lay mines off the Frisian Isles. Last, coincidentally, was 25 April 1945 bombing gun positions at Wangerooge, one of the Frisian Islands off the Dutch coast. There were sixteen Canadian bomber squadrons in Yorkshire.

Headquarters for No. 6 Group was at the seventy-five-room Allerton Park Castle near Knaresborough, requisitioned by the Air Ministry from Lord Mowbray and immortalised as 'Castle Dismal' by No. 6 Group's public relations officer.

This is a detailed description of a typical sortie, adapted from the 6th Bomber Group website: http://www.6bombergroup.ca/Sept44/Sept1744.html,

September 17, 1944

173 Halifaxes from 408, 415, 420, 424, 425, 426, 427, 429, 431, 432, 433, and 434 Squadrons were joined by 36 Lancasters from 419 and 428 squadrons on an attack of troop positions at Boulogne. The crews were over the target at between 2,000 and 10,000 feet,

Loading 500-lb high-explosive bombs onto the Whitleys of No. 58 Squadron at RAF Linton-on-Ouse in 1941.

releasing 2,280,000 lbs of high explosives. According to reports, bombing was accurate and these troops surrendered soon after.

P/O J. Tims from 415 Squadron returned without bombing on the master bomber's orders.

F/O G. Duncan from 419 Squadron returned early as the bombsight was u/s.

P/O W. MacDonald from 420 Squadron returned without bombing, as there were no T.I.'s. [Target Indicators –flares].

F/O W. Palidwar and F/O L. Wright from 424 Squadron returned without bombing, as there were no T.I.'s.

F/O J. King USAAF and crew flying Halifax III LW-117 coded QB-K swung on takeoff and crashed. The crew was not injured.

F/Lt G. Arbuckle was hit by flak outbound, F/O J. Morgan RCAF, the bomb aimer, was killed. They returned to base without bombing.

F/O J. Simard from 425 Squadron did not bomb, as they were too high over the target.

F/O J. Lasek from 429 Squadron returned without bombing, as there were no T.I.'s.

F/O J. Prentice RCAF and crew, flying Halifax III MZ-900 coded AL-K, was hit by flak. Both stbd engines were u/s and the stbd wing was on fire. This fire was put out only to start up in the port wing. The crew then bailed out into the English Channel.

The crew was later picked up by a Walrus. The rear gunner was slightly injured.

F/O M. Lanin did not bomb as there were no T.I.'s. On the return flight, this crew saw F/O J. Prentice in trouble and watched them bail out. The sea was smooth and they took a fix on the aircrew and flew to the English coast. They returned with a Walrus and two Spitfires for escort. Two of the crew were together in the water and the other five were about a mile away. After the walrus was on the water, they safely returned to base.

Sgt A. Stedman from 432 Squadron landed at Manston on return.

P/O H. Hawley from 434 Squadron returned without bombing, as the bomb doors would not open. They were also hit by flak, 3 feet of the port flap was shot off.

While the above crews were at Boulogne, 5 Halifaxes from 429 and 433 Squadrons were ordered on a Sea Search. All crews returned safely, but unsuccessful.

A Tucano jet trainer diving over RAF Linton-on-Ouse; formerly Harrogate Airport.

At the end of hostilities Linton took on a role transporting passengers and freight back to and from the UK – hence Harrogate Airport. In 1957 it became a Fighter Command station operating Hawker Hunters and other jets until it was closed briefly in 1957. It soon reopened as the home of No. 1 Flying Training School, responsible for training pilots for both the RAF and the Royal Navy.

Today, Linton-on-Ouse gives fast jet pilot training before pilots graduate onto Hawks at No. 4 FTS, RAF Valley in Wales. Weapon systems operators are also trained at Linton; the base is used by No. 642 VGS (Volunteer Gliding Squadron) to teach air cadets how to fly the Grob Vigilant aircraft.

In November 2008 Wing Commander Paul Gerrard, who is based at Linton, was involved in an amazing mid-air rescue. Sixty-five-year-old Jim O'Neill was flying a four-seater Cessna 182 from Scotland to Essex after a family holiday, when he had a stroke which caused him to go blind. Gerrard, who was on a training flight, located O'Neill's aircraft and over forty-five minutes, guided O'Neill to safety at Linton.

Fast jet training No. 72 squadron has been based at RAF Linton-on-Ouse since 2002, operating the Short Tucano T.1 for both RAF and RN Fleet Air Arm personnel. Prince William trained here. It remains one of the RAF's busiest bases.

The Army Foundation College

In 1924 the Boy's Technical Schools were opened by the War Office; in 1929 these were renamed Army Technical Schools (Boys). In 1947 they changed the name again to the Army Apprentices Schools and were finally renamed as the Army Apprentices Colleges in 1966. The Army Foundation College in Harrogate trains future soldiers from the infantry, armoured corps, artillery and elements of the Royal Logistic Corps; it is in Uniacke Barracks in Penny Pot Lane.

The Association of Harrogate Apprentices was reformed in 1999. Its role is to reunite anyone in any way associated with the Army Apprentice School, such as ex-apprentice tradesmen, permanent staff members, ex-NAAFI employees, civilian instructors etc. who served or worked on the establishment itself in such satellites as the YMCA or Salvation Army canteens. Training at the Army Foundation College includes:

- Fieldcraft – learning to live, eat and survive in the field.
- Skill at arms – learning to use the Army's infantry weapon, the SA80 A2.
- Fitness training – a structured programme to improve physical fitness with sessions in the gym as well as swimming, sports and other outdoor activities.
- Qualities of a soldier – learning about the Army's values and standards.
- Military knowledge – learning about the roles in the Army.
- Battlefield casualty drills – learning to treat casualties in a battlefield situation.
- Individual health – learning to live a healthy lifestyle.
- Education – Information Communication Technology qualification.

At any one time there are 1,300 soldiers under training with about 500 permanent staff.

The first British military presence on Penny Pot Lane was the 9th Field Training Regiment, Royal Artillery, who fired their guns on the moors near Blubberhouses. They were disbanded in 1943. Then came the 116th General Hospital of the United States Army, from 28 July 1944 to 11 May 1945, whose role it was to clear war casualties. Uniacke barracks was named after Lieutenant General Sir Herbert Uniacke KCB KCMG, an artillery officer (1866–1934). Penny Pot apparently comes from the time of the First World War, when soldiers would go out of camp to buy ale at the local farm for 'a penny a pot'.

Harrogate (Stonefall) Cemetery

A Commonwealth War Graves Commission burial ground for the dead of the First World War and the Second World War. As we have said, there were a number of RAF and Canadian Air Force bases in the vicinity during the Second World War; notably, No. 6 RCAF Bomber Group had headquarters at Allerton Park.

An area of the municipal cemetery was set aside for use as a war cemetery at the start of the war and received burials, mainly after July 1943, mostly for Canadian airman for the duration of the war. Burials are mainly from northern airfields and the military unit of the long-gone Harrogate General Hospital in Starbeck.

There are also burials of or memorials to twenty-three First World War troops here. A plaque in the cemetery records the names of twelve servicemen of the Second World War who were cremated rather than buried here. A special memorial commemorates six First World War troops whose graves are in local churchyards around Yorkshire and cannot be maintained by the commission.

Among the burials are three Canadians of the seven-man crew of a Lancaster bomber that crashed on Helmsley Moor on 17 May 1944. Five burials (all RCAF, but two were from the United States) in adjoining plots are of the crew of Halifax bomber which crashed into a railway bridge in Bishop Monkton on 15 April 1944.

Also, the Canadian crew of a Wellington which crashed near Oakworth on the night of 2 January 1944 taking off on a night training mission. The pilot, Flight Sergeant Ernest Glass, brought the aircraft down through low cloud and crashed into the hillside at Tewitt Hall Wood. The remains of the aircraft were cleared away and little remains today at the site of the crash except for the burnt and broken trees.

Harrogate's impeccably kept war cemetery: 988 graves, two-thirds of which are Royal Canadian Air Force, with others from the RAF and the Australian and New Zealand Air Forces.

RAF Menwith Hill – Lifting the Lid on Harrogate's Worst Kept Secret

A Royal Air Force station providing communications and intelligence services to the UK and the USA. The site, codename MOONPENNY, contains an extensive satellite ground station and is a communications intercept and missile warning site; it is probably the largest electronic monitoring station in the world. Until 2014 support services were provided by the USAF, No. 421 Air Base Group. Of the 1,800 employees in 2012, 400 were British and 1,200 were American employees of the NSA. The National Security Agency – an American government intelligence organization – is responsible for global monitoring, collection, and processing of information and data for foreign intelligence and counter-intelligence purposes. It is a ground station for a number of satellites operated by the US National Reconnaissance Office on behalf of the NSA, with antennae housed in large white radomes; it is alleged to be an element of the ECHELON system – 'a signals intelligence (SIGINT) collection and analysis network operated on behalf of the five signatory nations to the UKUSA Security Agreement — Australia, Canada, New Zealand, the United Kingdom, and the United States ('Five-Eyes').'

In the 1990s, British journalist Duncan Campbell and New Zealand journalist Nicky Hager alleged in Somebody's Listening that the US was exploiting ECHELON traffic for industrial espionage, rather than for military and diplomatic purposes. Examples alleged

RAF Menwith Hill, or should that be USAF Menwith Hill?

include the gearless wind turbine technology designed by the German firm Enercon, and the speech technology developed by the Belgian firm Lernout & Hauspie. The NSA admit to having spied on and intercepted the phone calls of Princess Diana until her death with Dodi Fayed in 1997. The NSA currently admits to holding 1,056 pages of classified information about the princess, which has been classified as top secret 'because their disclosure could reasonably be expected to cause exceptionally grave damage to the national security.' In the early 1990s, the NSA intercepted communications between the European aerospace company Airbus and Saudia, the Saudi national airline. In 1994, Airbus watched their $6 billion contract with Saudia evaporate after the NSA, acting as a whistleblower, reported that Airbus officials had been bribing Saudi officials to secure the contract. As a result, the American aerospace company McDonnell Douglas (now part of Boeing) won the multi-billion dollar contract instead of Airbus.

In March 2012 researcher Dr Steve Schofield produced a report titled 'Lifting the Lid on Menwith Hill', funded by the highly respected and authoritative Joseph Rowntree Charitable Trust and commissioned and published by the Yorkshire Campaign for Nuclear Disarmament. Schofield alleged that Menwith Hill was 'involved in drone attacks'. He said: 'The UK's providing a facility here that's involved in drone attacks that we know, from independent assessments, are killing and injuring thousands of civilians.' During the 2009 G20 London Summit, NSA specialists based at Menwith Hill attempted to target and decode the encrypted telephone calls of the Russian president Dmitry Medvedev.

Harrogate VC

Capt. Richard Kirby Ridgeway was born on 18 August 1848 in Oldcastle, County Meath, Ireland. On 22 November 1879, he was thirty-one years old, and a captain in the Bengal Staff Corps, 44th Gurkha Rifles (later 1/8th Gurkha Rifles), British Indian Army, during the Naga Hills Expedition. In the final assault on Konoma (near Kohima) that day, under heavy fire Captain Ridgeway rushed a barricade and attempted to tear down the planking surrounding it to enable him to effect an entrance. In doing so he was wounded severely in the right shoulder. For prestigious gallantry in the face of the enemy, he was awarded the Victoria Cross on 8 May 1880. He later rose to the rank of colonel. Ridgeway died at the age of seventy-six in Harrogate on 11 October 1924. He is buried in Lawnswood Cemetery, Adel.

I Never Knew that about Harrogate

- Thomas Sydenham (1624–1689), the father of British medicine, prescribed Harrogate's chalybeate waters for hysteria.
- Harrogate's invaluable impact of medicine does not end there: in 1893 local doctor George Oliver was the first to observe the effect of adrenaline on the circulation.
- Two years later, Dr Pritchard Roberts of Harrogate became the first British doctor to do his rounds using a motor car, in this case a Benz automobile.
- In 1894 Princess Alix of Hesse, granddaughter of Queen Victoria, came to Harrogate. She stayed at Cathcart House on West Park, the home of the Allen family, where she discovered that Mrs Allen had recently given birth to twins. To Alix this was a good omen and so she asked if she could be their godmother and that the girl be called Alix, after her, and the boy Nicholas, after the Cesarevitch of Russia to whom she was engaged to be married. The Princess attended the christening at St Peter's church and signed the Baptismal certificates. She also bought christening presents in Harrogate. A pair of Faberge gold cufflinks in the shape of the Imperial Russian Eagle set with diamonds and sapphires were given to Nicholas Allen as a confirmation present in 1910 from his godmother, the Czarina of Russia.
- In 1901 the population was 26,000. By 1951 the population of Harrogate was 50,000. Harrogate Theatre opened in 1900. In 1903 the Kursaal opened, renamed the Royal Hall in 1918. The war memorial was erected in 1923. Sun Pavilion and Sun Colonnade were built in 1933. After 1948, the NHS started referring patients to the Royal Baths for treatment; NHS funding ended in 1968. The Baths closed in 1969. The Royal Pump Room became a museum in 1953. Tewit Well was sealed in 1971 and Harrogate Conference Centre opened in 1982.
- Harrogate's Cold War bunker opened in Grove Road in 1958 on the site of a Second World War air-raid shelter and was manned by volunteers from the Royal Observation Corps who had to live within four minutes of the bunker – that being the length of the warning we would have got.
- The population at the last census for Harrogate District was 59,900. 9 per cent of the district's people were born outside of the UK; 5.3 per cent arrived in the UK between 2001 and 2011, both of these figures are the highest in North Yorkshire and reflect the invaluable, rich social and cultural diversity in Harrogate and its environs. In 2011 the

A busy day outside the Kursaal.

district's residents were overwhelmingly white (96.4 per cent); down from 99 per cent in 2001. People of Chinese origin account for the largest black or minority ethnic group (0.6 per cent), doubling in size from 2001 to 2011.

- In 2011 the most common non-English first languages spoken in the district were Polish (1,340) Chinese languages other than Cantonese and Mandarin (391); Hungarian (273); Tagalog/Filipino (233), and Russian (232).

- The district has a lower percentage of people younger than twenty-nine and a higher proportion aged forty-five and over. 27 per cent of the district's population is aged sixty and over (22.4 per cent nationally). The average age here is forty-two years old (thirty-nine nationally). In 2013, life expectancy (male): 79.6 (England: 78.6) (2008–2010). Female: 83.8 (England 82.6) (2008–2010).

- There are approximately 9,000 businesses within the Harrogate district occupying a workforce of approximately 75,000. The district's economy was estimated to be worth £2.7 billion in 2013; over a quarter of the North Yorkshire economy. In 2011, 69 per cent of the district's working-age population were economically active in 2011 (national average of 62 per cent). 40.8 per cent of the working-age population were in full-time employment (38.6 per cent nationally), 14.9 per cent were working part-time (13.7 per cent nationally) and 13.3 per cent were self-employed (9.8 per cent nationally).

- Harrogate has frequently been voted as one of the best places to live in the UK; in 2013 a poll of 40,000 people found that Harrogate was the happiest place to live in Great Britain. In 2013 Harrogate was voted the third most romantic destination in the world, finishing ahead of Paris, Rome and Vienna.

- On the downside, perhaps, along with Runnymede in Surrey, Harrogate people drink alcohol to more dangerous levels than anywhere else in the UK. 11 per cent of the district's drinking population consume at least twice the daily recommended amount of alcohol in a single drinking session; this is above the regional average of 10 per cent. Harrogate also has the highest concentration of drink drivers in the UK. 111 people were killed or seriously injured in road traffic incidents in 2012 – a 41 per cent reduction from 2011 (188 incidents). 16.4 per cent of households within the district do not own a car or van (compared to 25.8 per cent nationally).

- Harrogate was named as 'the online pornography capital of the country' when a BBC documentary revealed that residents from the town watched more adult material on their computers than anywhere else in the UK. The *Harrogate Advertiser* could not think of anybody to ask for a comment. Maybe all this explains why Harrogate was named as the 'happiest place' to live in the United Kingdom?

- Harrogate District Hospital has the best cancer care of any hospital in England according to the latest Cancer Patient Experience Survey, which measures cancer patients' experience while being treated at hospital. This includes, for example: if there were enough nurses on duty, whether patients were given enough support from health and social services when they left hospital, whether they were given the right emotional support or told about financial information.

- In 2012, 12.2 per cent of Year 6 children locally were classified as obese; much lower than the average for England of 19.2 per cent. The conception rate per 1,000 of the district's teenage girls was 2.5 between 2008 and 2010; compared with 7.4 nationally.

- In 2011/12, 91.2 per cent of the district's pupils gained 5+ A*-C GCSEs (80.5 per cent nationally). In 2011, the district's A-Level students averaged 810 points – compared with a national average of 728. In 2011 34 per cent of people over sixteen held a qualification above A-Level – well above the national average of 27 per cent. 17 per cent of over sixteen year olds have no qualifications (22.5 per cent nationally).
- Harrogate District has a coveted World Heritage Site: Fountains Abbey with Studley Royal, three historic battlefields and its award-winning parks and gardens. The district contains over 171 scheduled ancient monuments, forty-eight buildings of exceptional interest (Grade I) 113 of special interest (Grade II) and over 3,000 classified Grade III. The tourism and visitor economy represents around 25 per cent of the district's total economy, contributing £500 million annually and supporting some 23,000 jobs.

Religious Life

In the 2011 census, 68.6 per cent of the district's population were Christians (compared with 59.4 per cent nationally); 30 per cent of the district either stated they did not have a religion or did not answer the question. The remaining 1.4 per cent of the district were Muslim (0.4 per cent), Buddhist (0.3 per cent), Jewish (0.2 per cent), or of other faiths (0.5 per cent).

- There are between thirty-five and forty churches in Harrogate at any one time. The history of Christianity in Harrogate dates back to the fifteenth century with early chapels in around The Stray. St John's chantry chapel was founded in 1439, later becoming Christ Church. Its bell now tolls in the tower of West Park United Reformed church (previously the Victoria Avenue Congregational church). Christ Church on The Stray was the first purpose-built church building in Harrogate, originating as a church plant from St John's, Knaresborough, and then developing into a separate parish. Christ Church later planted St Peter's in the town centre, St John's, Bilton, and St Andrew's, Starbeck. St Robert's Roman Catholic Church (with a chapel at St John Fisher Catholic High School) is the largest single church in the town.

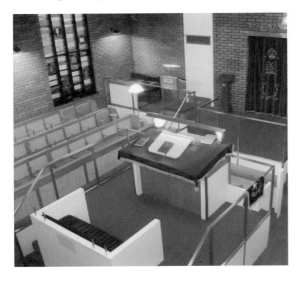

Harrogate Hebrew Congregation shul.

- The Harrogate Islamic Association is based in the town; the nearest mosque is Leeds Grand Mosque. Kagyu Dechen Dzong Buddhist Centre is in Granville Road.
- The Harrogate Hebrew Congregation was established in 1918; a synagogue was opened in St Mary's Walk in 1925. The current building was built in 1968 and holds up to 200 worshippers. There are approximately 180 interments or re-interments from 1964 to 2014 in Stonefall Cemetery. In 2004 there were 327 members of the Harrogate Jewish community according to *The Jewish Year Book 2005*.

Twinning

Currently, Harrogate is twinned with:

- Bagnères-de-Luchon, France (since 1952)
- Barrie, Canada (since 2013)
- Harrogate, a small town in Tennessee, United States
- Wellington, New Zealand

The Harrogate Hoard

In 2007, two metal detectorists uncovered the Harrogate hoard, a tenth-century Viking treasure hoard, near the town. The British Museum described it as the most important find of its type in Britain for 150 years. It consists of 617 silver coins and sixty-five other items, including ornaments, ingots and precious metal, all hidden in a gilt silver vessel lined with gold from around 900 and decorated with 'vines, leaves and six hunting scenes showing lionesess, stags, and a horse'. The vessel was probably used to hold communion bread for a wealthy church or monastery in northern France and seems to have been acquired either in a Viking raid or as tribute. The vessel was buried in a lead chest. A rare gold arm ring and hacksilver (fragments of cut metal sometimes used as currency) were also found. These coins bear Islamic, Christian and pre-Christian Norse pagan symbols: 'some of the coins mixed Christian and pagan imagery, shedding light on the beliefs of newly Christianized Vikings.'

Harrogate's special twin since 1952: Bagnères-de-Luchon.

The hoard may have belonged to a wealthy Viking leader during the unrest that followed the conquest of the Viking kingdom of Northumbria in 927 by the Anglo-Saxon king Athelstan (924–939). The hoard included objects from many places: including Samarkand in present-day Uzbekistan, North Africa, Afghanistan, Russia, Ireland, Scandinavia, and other areas of continental Europe, 'illustrating the breadth of the Vikings' travels and trade connections'. The hoard is in the Yorkshire Museum, York.

8. Harrogate's Hidden Villages

Starbeck and its Spa

In the seventeenth century, Knaresborough was known to physicians and health-seekers as 'the Knaresborough Spa', because it was a popular base for 'taking the waters' long before Harrogate had developed. This is shown by various publications, especially by Dr Deane's *Spadacrene Anglica* (1626), which recommends those staying in Knaresborough to visit not only mineral springs such as the Tewit Well and the Old Sulphur Well, but also those at Starbeck, and the Dropping Well and St Robert's Well and St Mungo's Well at Copgrove. Long after the term 'Knaresborough Spa' had been forgotten, it was applied to the renewed development at Starbeck.

This, of course, was because Knaresborough Spa was actually at Starbeck, on land which had been included in the boundary of Knaresborough by the 1778 Enclosure Act. The revival of an earlier spa here was promoted mainly through the enthusiasm of the Knaresborough chemist Michael Calvert and Dr Peter Murray. A public meeting was held in Knaresborough Town Hall in March 1822, forming a trust with a hundred shares, and two months later the foundation stone of a new pump room was laid by the 'Masons of England' following a procession from the Elephant & Castle, on the high street. By 1828, a suite of baths had been added for both warm and cold bathing. It was claimed of those who regularly drank the spa water – both sulphur and chalybeate – that 'the

Charlie Pyne's bus garage in Camwell Road, Starbeck in the '50s. (http://www .old-bus-photos.co.uk/ wp-content/themes/ Old-Bus-Photos/ articles/w_pyne_ starbeck/w_pyne_ starbeck.php; Keith Todd)

Idyllic Starbeck.

digestion becomes amended, the bowels and kidneys perform their functions in a more regular manner ... and the skin itself gradually assumes a natural and healthy state.' Knaresborough Spa never managed to rival the well-established mineral wells of High and Low Harrogate, with their superior accommodation, and by about 1890 it had closed down. Some of the early buildings can still be seen near the Star Beck, on Spa Lane, including the later Prince of Wales Baths (1870). The term 'Knaresborough Spa' was also used to describe Knaresborough itself in the seventeenth century.

Blind Jack of Knaresborough, and Harrogate
Blind Jack had connexions with Starbeck and Harrogate. Blind Jack is the nickname of John Metcalf, who was born in 1717 in a Knaresborough cottage (demolished in about 1768) near the parish church and was a true jack of all trades. He went to school aged four, but at the age of six he was afflicted by smallpox, which left him completely blind. An intelligent lad with prodigious determination and energy, he led an active life tree-climbing, swimming, hunting and gambling. At the age of fifteen, he was appointed fiddler at the Queen's Head in High Harrogate. Later, he earned money as a guide (working mainly at night-time), eloped with Dolly Benson, daughter of the landlord of the Royal Oak (later the Granby), and in 1745 marched as a musician to Scotland, leading Captain Thornton's 'Yorkshire Blues' to fight Bonnie Prince Charlie's rebels.

Blind Jack is best known for his work as a civil engineer, a pioneer of road building. His extensive travels and the stage-coach he ran between York and Knaresborough had acquainted him with the appalling state of English roads. Soon after the passing of a new Turnpike Act in 1752, he obtained a contract for building (with his gang of workmen) a three-mile stretch of road between Ferrensby and Minskip. Then he built part of the road from Knaresborough to Harrogate, including a bridge over the Starbeck, and went on to complete around 180 miles of road in Yorkshire, Lancashire and Derbyshire. The specially constructed via-meter he used to measure his roads can be seen in Knareborough's Courthouse Museum.

Following Dolly's death in 1778, he went to live with a married daughter in Spofforth. Here, after many active years in engineering and as a violin player, he died in 1810, leaving behind four children, twenty grandchildren and ninety great and great-great grandchildren. A tombstone in Spofforth churchyard pays tribute to the remarkable achievements of 'Blind Jack of Knaresborough', and he was commemorated with a sealed bronze statue in Knaresborough Market Place by Barbara Asquith in 2009.

Starbeck and the Railways

The railways were critical to the rise of Starbeck. When they came in 1848 they brought with them a corn mill, malt house and water bottling plant. The population expanded rapidly, with most families owing their livelihood in some way or another to the railway. But it all started to decline in the '50s. In 1951 the Pateley Bridge line closed to passenger traffic and the loop line to Pannal (under Crimple Viaduct) closed completely. In 1959 the engine shed and marshalling yard closed. In 1967 the passenger service to Ripon was came to an end. The last goods train travelled the old Leeds to Thirsk railway line from Starbeck to Northallerton on 9 October 1969, leaving only the current Harrogate Line to and from York.

Henry Peacock

Of the two public houses on the high street, the Prince of Wales and the Henry Peacock, the latter was named after the master of the local workhouse during the nineteenth century and is currently closed. Full details, such as they are, can be found at institutions.org.uk.

An extract from *Starbeck – A Journey Through the Past* by Stephen G. Abbott, which begins as follows:

> Henry Peacock was born in poverty, and spent his life not quite getting out of it. He first came to Starbeck in 1825 with his wife Elizabeth, as master and matron of the workhouse, for a joint salary of £50 a year. After having run the Aldborough and Boroughbridge workhouse for the previous three years, the Peacocks were noted to have viewed Harrogate as an opportunity to 'better themselves'.

Harrogate Railway Athletic F.C.

The club actually plays in Starbeck and was founded in 1935; it currently is in the Evo-Stick Northern Premier League Division One North. The club was founded when workers from Starbeck LNER locomotive shed formed an adult team to play in the Harrogate & District League. In 1946 the side consisted entirely of railway workers and reached the British Railways National Cup Final.

This prompted the club to look for a ground of their own, but they stayed at Station View when LNER said that they would lend the club the £1,500 they need necessary to purchase a site, on condition that Starbeck's 300 rail workers would agree to have 1*d* a week stopped from their wages to finance the repayments. More than enough volunteers signed up. In 1949 they won their league championships plus all the local cups: they were victorious in all twenty-four league matches with a goal tally of 150 goals to 29 against.

In the 2002/3 they reached the second round of the FA Cup before losing to Bristol City 3-1. In 2007/8, Railway once again reached the second round of the FA Cup after beating Harrogate rivals Harrogate Town 2-1 in the fourth preliminary round followed by a 2-0 win over Droylsden. Railway lost 3-2 to Mansfield Town in the second round, which was televised live on Match of the Day. The club finished eighth in the 2014/15 season with sixty-seven points from forty-two games.

Goldsborough

Goldsborough Hall was built around 1620 for Sir Richard Hutton, acting Lord Chief Justice; it was later remodelled in the 1750s by architects Robert Adam and John Carr of York.

During the Civil War, the house was forcibly occupied by Oliver Cromwell's troops in 1644 while they besieged Knaresborough Castle. Sir Richard Hutton the Younger fought at

Goldsborough Hall was the first family home of Mary, Princess Royal and Countess of Harewood, and Viscount Lascelles, Henry Lascelles, 6th Earl of Harewood after their marriage in 1922. The picture shows their son, George Henry Hubert Lascelles, 7th Earl of Harewood, christened at Goldsborough church on 25 March 1923, the service was attended by George V and Queen Mary and officiated by Cosmo Lang, the Archbishop of York.

GOLDSBOROUGH: ENTRANCE TO VILLAGE.

The gates at
Goldsborough Hall.

the battle of Marston Moor in 1644 and was killed at Sherburn-in-Elmet in 1645. The hall was the first family home of Mary, Princess Royal, Countess of Harewood and Viscount Lascelles, Henry Lascelles, 6th Earl of Harewood after their marriage in 1922.

A Viking hoard was unearthed in 1859 during building work near Goldsborough church. Coins and artefacts dating from 700 to 1050 were found in a lead chest including fragments of Viking brooches and arm-rings, together with thirty-nine coins. It is one of the largest collections ever discovered in the UK and is now held at the British Museum.

Pannal

With origins going back to the Bronze Age, Pannal had become a thriving market village with weekly markets and an annual four-day fair by the early fourteenth century. The parish of Pannal covered a large area, including Beckwith, Beckwithshaw, Brackenthwaite and Low Harrogate. In 1894 Low Harrogate became part of Harrogate, and in 1937 the village of Pannal was also added to Harrogate. This left the village outside the civil parish of Pannal, a confusing situation, the like of which only local councillors could contrive. The bungling prevailed until 2010 when the civil parish was renamed Beckwithshaw.

Spacey Houses is on the other side of the Leeds–Harrogate road, the A61. The recently demolished Spacey Houses pub was on the Pannal side of the road, named after the coaching inn on the Spacey Houses side which had been converted into a farm house.

Follifoot

The name is derived from Old Norse translating meaning 'place of the horse fight', the beginning of a long association with horse sports. The earliest record is Pholifet from the twelfth century. Anglo-Saxon remains have been discovered in and around the village and an Anglian cross stands at the crossroads at the top of the village. In the nineteenth century the village was a thriving community with its flax industry, tannery, tailors, joiners, a wheelwright, cordwainer and blacksmiths.

One of Britain's greatest pub signs is that of the Squinting Cat in Pannal, built around 1720 as a smithy but converted to a coaching inn, in which the dining room was used to repair coaches. The name derives from an old lady who lived there and spent her days squinting out of the window at people. So, in 1930 when the pub was refurbished it was called the Squinting Cat. It has been subsequently ruined by further (unsympathetic) renovation.

The White House at Mill Lane, Pannal; the building to the left was a brewery taken over by Kirkstall Brewery during the First World War, their beer exported to New Zealand and Australia on Kirkstall's own ships, the *SS Charante* and the *SS Kirkstall*.

Digging for victory in Pannal during the Second World War.

A dual cooking and writing lesson at Pannal school during the Second World War.

Ripley

Ripley is essentially Ripley Castle. However, the village itself is not without interest. A nineteenth-century member of the incumbent Ingilby family tore down the old village and rebuilt it modeled after an Alsatian village with a hôtel-de-ville-style town hall. The castle and the parish church were unaffected by the 'reconstruction'.

The village of Follifoot with the arched entrance to Ruddick Park in the background.

Ripley and Ripley Castle.

Ripley and Ripley Castle.

Ripley Castle II.

"Photo by M. E. Mitchell & Co."

Ripley Castle

The castle dates from the fourteenth century, and has been the home of the Ingilby family for 700 years. The present owner is Sir Thomas Ingilby, 6th Baronet and the twenty-eighth generation. The castle, which is noted for, among other things, a priest hole discovered by accident in 1964, lies in landscaped grounds and ornamental lakes.

King Edward III stayed several times nearby in Knaresborough Castle, most notably in January 1328 after his marriage to Queen Philippa in York. There are references to Edward breeding horses in the 'Park de la Haye' (Haya Park) and hunting deer and boar in the Forest of Knaresborough. In 1355, he was attacked by a boar he had wounded, and was thrown from his horse. His life was saved by Thomas Ingilby of Ripley Castle, who killed the animal; Ingilby later received a knighthood, and a boar's head was henceforth included in the Ingilby arms. The following is adapted from the Ingilby history http://ingilbyhistory.ripleycastle.co.uk/.

When Sir Thomas Ingleby (1290–1352) married Edeline Thwenge in 1308, her baggage included a modest dowry: Ripley Castle and its surrounding estates. In 1318 the marauding Scots, under Sir James 'Black' Douglas, plundered the region mercilessly, destroying 140 of the 160 houses in nearby Knaresborough. In 1319 bovine plague killed almost all of the cattle in the region, leaving thousands of locals destitute and milk in short supply. In 1349 the Black Death struck, wiping out almost half of the local population.

The Ingilbys were implicated with nine of the eleven principal conspirators of the gunpowder plot. The mother of Robert and Thomas Wyntour was an Ingleby. The plotters had spent the week before 5 November at Ripley, buying horses from the surrounding district. Sir William and his son were arrested and charged with treason, but were, astonishingly, acquitted of all charges.

Sir William Ingleby (1594–1652) supported Charles I throughout the Civil War, raising a troop of cavalry to fight under Prince Rupert of the Rhine. He fought at Marston Moor, alongside his sister, 'Trooper' Jane Ingleby, and lived to fight another day and made for the safety of the priest hole in Ripley Castle. He was followed by Oliver Cromwell leaving his sister in control ... She at first refused to let him into the castle but later, he was allowed to enter and spend the night there, guarded at pistol point by Jane.

Sir William Amcotts Ingilby (1783–1854) was a great eccentric, a drinker, gambler and bounder. Believing that his tenants and workers should be well housed in the industrial revolution, Sir William demolished the entire village and rebuilt it as a model estate village, copying something he had observed in Alsace Lorraine. Instead of a town hall, Ripley has a 'Hôtel de Ville' – unique in England. He died without heir and left the estate to his cousin Henry, telling him that he was doing so because 'I don't believe that you are any longer the canting hypocrite I took you for.'

Harrogate Timeline

1332 – Earliest surviving documentary evidence of the name 'Harrogate'.

1399 – The whole of Harrogate became royal property when the possessions of the Duchy of Lancaster merged with the English Royal Crown.

1496 – Appointment of the earliest known Harrogate Constable, Robert Mathew.

1596 – Dr Bright dubbed Harrogate 'The English Spa' the first place to be called that in England.

1626 – Publication of Edmund Deane's *Spadacrene Anglica* – the first nationwide publicity for Harrogate Spa.

1631 – A second well was discovered close to the Tewit Well by Michael Stanhope. This well was a 'Chalybeate', or Iron Spring, and known as St John's Well.

1680 – Harrogate growing as a magnet for visitors who come for its medicinal wells; eighty-eight springs were found altogether – thirty-six in the Valley Gardens.

1749 – A chapel dedicated to St John is built to cater for increasing religious needs.

1778 – The Enclosures Act for the Forest of Knaresborough ensured that the public wells would remain accessible by persuading Parliament to leave 200 acres of the forest, which included the principle springs, unenclosed. The Stray is an invaluable asset to Harrogate. Water from the spa was bathed in as well as drunk.

1786 – Wedderburn House is built.

1788 – First theatre is built in Harrogate.

1805 – The Promenade Rooms were built and opened in 1806.

1806 – Lord Byron stayed at the Crown Hotel. There is now a plaque outside to commemorate his visit.

1826 – Bath Hospital is built.

1831 – Christ Church is consecrated. Harrogate is growing and has a population of 4,000.

1835 – Johnathan Shutt Junior, owner of the Old Swan Hotel, discovered that his neighbour Joseph Thackwray, manager of the Crown Hotel, intended to build a well, yielding sulphur water and drain the flow of the public well. He already owned private wells and private bathing establishments.

1841 –Because of this and other acts of vandalism to the wells, the Harrogate Improvements Act of 1841 was approved. Local senior citizens and local hoteliers petitioned for an Act of Parliament to create a body of Improvement Commissioners to ensure that nobody pirated the precious waters.

1842 – Royal Pump Room is built.

1846 – The first water company is formed.

1847 – Harrogate gets gas lighting.

1848 – The railway reaches Harrogate. Trains boost health tourism and the growth of the town.

1884 – Harrogate gets its first mayor and corporation.

1887 – The first public library opens in Harrogate; the Valley Gardens were established to commemorate the Golden Jubilee of Queen Victoria's reign.

1895 – Magnesia Well is discovered.

1897 – Harrogate goes electric. The Royal Baths opens.

1900 – Harrogate Theatre opens.

1901 – Harrogate now has a population of about 26,000.

1903 – Royal Hall is built.

1914 – Harrogate opens its doors for the rehabilitation of wounded servicemen.

1923 – The war memorial is erected.

A beautiful print of Christ Church on The Stray.

The memorial service for Edward VII in May 1910.

The proclamation of George V outside the Royal Baths in May 1910, with the Spa Concert Rooms in the background.

Peace celebrations in 1919 showing a tea laid on the for the poorer Harrogate children.

1926 – The missing crime novelist, Agatha Christie, turned up at the Old Swan Hotel (Harrogate Hydropathic as it was known then). Overwork had caused a breakdown; a poster at Waterloo railway station promoting Harrogate induced Christie to travel to the town.

1929 – On one morning it was recorded that 1,500 drinks of sulphur water were served from the Royal Pump Room.

1933 – Sun Pavilion and Sun Colonnade are built.

1951 – The population of Harrogate is now 50,000.

1953 – The Royal Pump Room becomes a museum.

1969 – The Royal Baths close for all treatments except the Turkish Baths; Harrogate ceased to be a spa town in the true sense of the word.

1971 – Tewit Well is sealed.

1977 – The film *Agatha*, starring Dustin Hoffman and Vanessa Redgrave, shot at the Old Swan Hotel and in Harrogate.

1982 – Harrogate Conference Centre opens.

1982 – The Eurovision Song Contest held in Harrogate.

2008 – Royal Hall is refurbished.

2014 – Tour de France races through Harrogate.

Acknowledgements

Thanks to the staff at the Royal Baths Chinese Restaurant; Sarah Wells at Bettys & Taylors of Harrogate Ltd; Steve Lewis at York Press. Phil Davison, Leeds Historical Expedition Society, for the quotation regarding Brunswick Tunnel and air-raid shelter; likewise Phil Catford of 'Subterranea Britannica'; Peter Arnett, Press Officer/Programme Editor/Webmaster/Official Photographer, Harrogate Town AFC; Helen McGlynn, Literature Festivals Co-ordinator, Harrogate International Festivals for the Old Peculier image and the logo for Harrogate Crime Writing Festival.

Other related books by Paul Chrystal:

- *Harrogate Through Time*
- *Knaresborough Through Time*
- *Vale of York Through Time*
- *A Children's History of Harrogate & Knaresborough*
- *An A-Z of Knaresborough History Revised Edition*
- *Secret Knaresborough*
- *Changing Scarborough*
- *Secret York*

96

The coloured multi-view card embossed with gold foil was written in July 1918 by a rather homesick Edith to Miss Annie Easby in Stockton-on-Tees. Edith has come to Harrogate (No. 4 Granville Road) with 'two young ladies from Middlesbro'. Despite having a good time, 'she would rather be home all the same'. She finishes the card off on something of an Alan Sherman *Camp Granada* note: 'Harrogate is a lovely place – plenty of swanks'.

- *Tea: A Very British Beverage*
- *Harrogate Pubs, including Knaresborough* (forthcoming)
- *Coffee: A Drink for the Devil* (forthcoming)

For a full list please go to www.paulchrystal.com.
Unless acknowledged otherwise, all photography is © Paul Chrystal.